LEADING
from YOUR
STRENGTHS

John Trent
Rodney Cox

LEADING
from YOUR
STRENGTHS

BUILDING CLOSE-KNIT MINISTRY TEAMS

PUBLISHING GROUP

NASHVILLE, TENNESSEE

ISBN: 978-0-8054-3061-5

Published by B&H Publishing Group
Nashville, Tennessee

Dewey Decimal Number: 259
Subject Heading: MINISTRY \ CHURCH WORK

7 8 9 10 11 12 13 14 15   14 13 12 11 10 09 08

This book is dedicated to Bill and Dave Bonnstetter, a father and son team who have dedicated their lives to helping others understand and use their unique strengths and who have supported our efforts to do the same. May God richly bless both of you.

Acknowledgments

I'd especially like to thank Doug Barram, Bob Leenhouts, and Doug Childress for the way they've encouraged me to lead from my strengths for years, in spite of knowing and seeing my weaknesses. Special thanks too to Cindy, my life partner, and to Kari and Laura, who are precious gifts to us as well as being wonderful, godly daughters.

—John Trent

I will be forever grateful to Bruce and Carol Mazzare for introducing me to the principles of personality and for their love and wisdom. I'd like to thank John and Cindy Trent for their creativity and love for the Lord and for taking a risk in developing new ways to help people build strong, God-honoring relationships. I want to thank my wonderful wife, Elizabeth, whose unfailing support through trials and triumphs has allowed me to follow my dreams, and my daughters, Ashley and Amy, who bring great joy to our lives.

—Rodney Cox

We would like to thank Patrick Poole for his contributions to this book. We would also like to thank Dr. John Michael, Brent Rowland, and the rest of the Leading From Your Strengths® team for all of their hard work.

Contents

Chapter One

Ministries Hanging in the Balance

★

IT'S 10:20 P.M. AND A PIERCING winter wind refuses to relinquish its iron grip on an early spring night. Kevin sits alone in his office. Normally this senior pastor of a growing church would have raced home from work, wolfed down his dinner, and gotten ready for a weekly small-group study at his house. That study was a high point of the week for Kevin and his wife, Karen.

Not tonight.

Tonight, Karen got a call saying Kevin was staying late and to go on without him. The florescent lights from his office shine out onto a dark, empty parking lot as he sits at his computer and struggles with the words on the screen.

Kevin isn't wrestling with the right phrases for Sunday's sermon; he's working on his resumé. In fact, he's seriously thinking about getting out of pastoral ministry altogether.

For twelve years at his last church, Kevin experienced a fruitful, fulfilling ministry. He'd built a small, close-knit staff; worked well with his deacons; and been able to focus on preaching and teaching his flock. Now, after only *a year and a half* at his new church, Kevin had become so frustrated—so deeply angry with Rick, the senior music minister—he dreaded even coming into the office. That wasn't the worst. His internal tension level had risen so high because of the conflict that it often overflowed at home. He snapped at his kids and even pushed back from his wife.

1

Day and night the emotional burden of these unresolved issues weighed on Kevin like a seventy-five-pound pack. That weight became a constant feeling of failure—a nagging heaviness that he had let down his family, his God, and especially the people in his flock. As Kevin typed his resumé, struggling to paint a positive picture of his gifts and strengths, he thought about adding words like *hypocrite, loser, failure,* and *quitter.*

How could he talk about reconciliation and forgiveness on Sunday and yet have so many unresolved issues with Rick? It wasn't from a lack of prayer or face-to-face effort to make things right. He'd never tried harder in his life to get on the same page with another person. But these two committed Christians were polar opposites. On every issue—from the look of the bulletin to the style of music on Sunday—they had different points of view. And every time Kevin tried to bridge the gap and make things better, he seemed to make things worse.

You might ask, "As the senior pastor, couldn't he just fire the source of all this frustration?" Kevin knew this wasn't an option. There were no ethical or moral problems and no question that Rick worked hard and wanted the best for the church. This, added to the fact that Rick had been at the church for seventeen years and Kevin less than two, meant that Rick went with the furniture.

His unsought adversary wasn't going anywhere.

Which was why on this dark, windy night, Kevin thought of going somewhere—anywhere—where there wasn't so much pain.

STEPPING INTO A POWER STRUGGLE

Sandy was a new Christian who had answered the call to be part of a volunteer committee for her church's women's ministry. When the Sunday bulletin announced that they were looking for someone with marketing and promotional ideas to help with special events, Sandy felt God's Spirit tap on her shoulder. After all, she was a full partner at a noted advertising agency and had won industry awards for running entire brand campaigns. Using her marketing skills to serve the Lord on a committee at church seemed right down her alley—until she discovered the back-alley politics going on in the group.

The politics began before Sandy even got inside for the first meeting! That's because a lady named Jennifer met her in the parking lot as soon as she stepped out of her car. Between the parking lot and the meeting room, Jennifer quickly explained to Sandy "the way things operated" on the committee. Of course, during the first break in their meeting, another vocal lady named Michelle made a point of cornering Sandy. It was clear Michelle was on a mission to tell her "the way things happened" in the group from her standpoint.

For years Sandy had walked into clients' offices where there was an obvious culture of conflict. She expected that in the rough-and-tumble corporate advertising world, but she never thought she'd see such intense lobbying and politics inside a church. While their focus was to be on helping women in the church love and serve Jesus, the friction in the room was equal to or worse than anything she'd seen in a corporate meeting. Instead of getting to use her strengths to serve, Sandy and the other committee members basically watched Jennifer, the irresistible force, spar with Michelle, the immovable object, from the opening prayer to the closing prayer. The constant verbal and nonverbal tug-of-war between these two kept anything positive from happening in the group. So much so that after bottling up her emotions for weeks, one night Sandy blew up and walked out of the meeting.

As she started her car in the church parking lot, brokenhearted and discouraged, Sandy vowed she'd never volunteer for anything at her church again.

RUSHING TO REJECTION

And then there was Dan, the only single man that this historic church had ever asked to serve as a deacon. He was honored when he'd been asked to become a deacon, and he thought that his accounting skills would help resolve some of the financial difficulties he knew the church faced.

The day before his first deacons' meeting, he received a package containing the most recent financial audit, a set of deacons meeting minutes for the past three years, and a copy of the proposed annual budget that the deacons were to vote on the following day. What he saw shocked him. For three years running, the ministry expenses had exceeded donations by more than 20 percent each year. Virtually every area of the ministry was consistently over budget, and the shortfalls were being covered by a fund that had actually been designated for other purposes.

What concerned Dan most was that the deacons had approved every departmental request for more money without a single dissenting vote. He spent most of that evening pouring over the audit, the minutes, and the budget details with a fine-tooth comb. Then, in a burst of energy, he outlined a plan.

At Dan's first deacons meeting, barely five minutes into his tenure, Dan raised his hand. Breaking into a discussion that had just started on hiring a new staff person, he used that new expense as a way to launch into a litany of proposed accounting and spending reforms. He even detailed program and personnel cuts he felt were necessary, with some of the people affected by his cuts in the room. By the time he finished his proposal twenty minutes later, you could hear a pin drop in the conference room.

With a "Thank you, Dan, but let's look at what's on our agenda tonight," the deacon chairman finally broke the heavy silence. Two hours later Dan walked out of the meeting feeling nothing but disappointment and rejection.

Instead of feeling welcome or that his ideas had merit, the only thing Dan felt was resentment and cold stares.

WHAT IF THINGS REALLY COULD CHANGE?

If you've ever worked or volunteered at any level in a Christian organization, church, small group, or association, you can probably identify with at least some of the feelings of isolation, frustration, and disappointment expressed in the three lives above. In far too many ministry teams, what's common is discord and division rather than the unity of the Spirit. Instead of exercising our spiritual gifts and callings, many times we feel pressured and stressed, frustrated instead of fulfilled.

But what if we told you that the solution to these common conflicts was closer than you ever dreamed?

What if there really was a way for a team to elimate predictable problems before they happen? What if there was an effective solution for conflict that already exists between team members? What if you really could put people in positions on a team that matched their strengths so that they felt useful and energized? What if there was a way to keep the focus of a ministry team on ministry and serving the Lord with honor and excellence instead of division and defeat?

The Leading From Your Strengths® process is all about knowing your God-given strengths, understanding and valuing the strengths of others, and blending the differences to reduce frustration, increase closeness, decrease conflict, and dramatically increase caring and commitment on your team. It's about each person you labor with understanding and using his or her strengths instead of feeling used or unnecessary.

LOOKING BACK AT WHAT TIPPED
THE BALANCE TOWARD CLOSENESS

In 1 Corinthians 12:18, the apostle Paul concludes his discussion of how God's people are like members of a body by stating, "But now God has placed the parts, each one of them, in the body just as He wanted." We believe that is absolutely true today. The group of people you're working with isn't the result of a random coincidence. These people you're working with are part of God's story for your life. That's an amazing thing to think about in itself. It's also why investing time in building a healthy, functional, effective, empowering team is essential, not optional. By working through this book as a team and having each person take his or her Leading From Your Strengths® assessment, which will come along later in the book, our prayer is that your team will bear more fruit, work together more freely, and use the collective strengths of the team more effectively than ever before.

Which takes us back to Kevin, Sandy, and Dan, three people whose ministries hung in the balance as we began this chapter. They were also three people who, during a turning point in their lives, used the Leading From Your Strengths® process outlined in this book.

For Kevin, working through the concepts in this book and the results from his Leading From Your Strengths® assessment made working at church fun and fulfilling again, and he never did finish that resumé. But what amazed him was what happened with Rick, his senior staff adversary. In the process of working through the material, they not only turned the corner on their long-standing animosity, but their relationship turned into a genuine friendship!

For Sandy, a wise pastoral staff person, who saw the women's ministry melting down, had the entire committee go through the material presented in this book. That process brought Sandy back to the table, broke up the Michelle-Jennifer logjam, tore down the walls other team members had put up, and set the stage for a revitalized women's ministry at their church! We hear this time and time again. The insights gained through the Leading From Your Strengths® process can break down barriers to closeness and growth in committees and teams and among individuals.

And for Dan while sweeping changes were eventually made to the church's accounting practices, going through the Leading From Your Strengths® material with the deacons spurred dramatic changes in Dan's personal life as well. As a part of the deacon ministry team, Dan saw some things about himself that led to real changes in how he approached problems and people in general. Instead of a being a full-throttle bulldozer, Dan actually started listening and asking questions instead of attacking. He became an effective, much appreciated deacon for two terms. Even more, what Dan learned in relating to others in his ministry team helped him become a better, more sensitive person overall—including the way it spilled over into a relationship he had with a woman at the church who later became his wife.

Chapter Two

Getting a Feel for What Follows

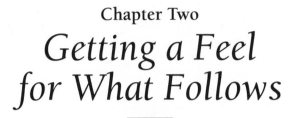

THE LEADING FROM YOUR STRENGTHS® material that follows comes from a study of predictable behavioral traits, as well as forty-five combined years of ministry *and* corporate team-building experience by the authors. Because we believe that being a part of your ministry team is a part of God's story for your life, we've based this book, and the Leading From Your Strengths® assessment, on three core principles.

1. Understanding your own God-given strengths. This is a key to growth, change, and finding your place on the team where God has placed you.
2. Recognizing and respecting the God-given strengths of others on your team. This is a key to the commitment of each team member to each other.
3. Blending differences among team members and harnessing each person's unique strengths. This results in greater effectiveness and productivity for your team.

In more than two decades of continuous hands-on involvement with ministry teams of all shapes and sizes, virtually every problem situation we've seen involves some breach of these core principles.

While lots of words will follow, we'd like to begin by giving you a feel for what can happen in your life and ministry by working through the Leading From Your Strengths® process. This isn't a busywork exercise but something we urge you to do right now

as a way of gaining a tangible picture of what Leading From Your
Strengths® is all about.

On the first line below, or on another piece of paper if you
prefer, we'd like you to sign your first, middle, and last name,
using your nondominant hand. If you're right-handed, put
a pen or pencil in your left hand, or vise versa if you're
left-handed.

_____

Now, switch your pen back to your dominant hand and sign
your first, middle, and last name as you would at the end of
a letter or other document.

_____

Did you feel the difference in those two tasks? Which took
longer? Which took more focused thought and energy? Which
was easier and quicker? Which took almost no conscious
thought and seemed like second nature?

What you just did is get a feel for how Leading From Your
Strengths® can change you and your team into a faster, more
efficient, more productive unit. That's because the net result of
working through this book and taking your Leading From Your
Strengths® assessment is to have each person on your team "put
the pen in their _right_ hand" when it comes to the tasks and challenges set before them. So where do we begin this process?

With a helicopter ride, of course!

A Flyover of What Lies Ahead

Picture that you're climbing into a helicopter near Lee's
Ferry, Arizona. If that tiny town doesn't sound familiar, you're
just miles from the Grand Canyon and right on the banks of the
Colorado River. It's a beautiful early summer's day, and you're
moments away from taking off on your first helicopter ride.
Actually, this isn't just _any_ helicopter. This is an AS350 A-Star
Jetcopter that seats six people, plus the pilot, and allows for

180-degree views in air-conditioned comfort. We'll pretend there are actually two of these beautiful deep blue Jetcopters carrying your entire ministry team on a flyover of what will become an adventure of a lifetime, a raft trip down the Colorado River.

As the jet engine whines and you lift off (you are seated in the right front seat next to the pilot, of course), you soon are hovering over a small building on the edge of the Colorado River. That building is your River School where the white-water rafting company will introduce you to your guide and teach you the ways of the river. Then, beyond the school, you can see a dozen huge steel-gray Avon rafts tied up. Your whole team will soon be assigned one of these rafts.

The Colorado River is wide and calm as you start your fly-by of the water road you'll follow, but that calm soon changes. In fact, four times on your flight, your pilot hovers over key "transitions" in the river—better known as four major rapids. At each major rapid the pilot tips the rotor up, and the nose of the Jetcopter goes down, allowing you to see that these are different rapids that will have to be tackled in different ways. Finally, you fly over the place where the boats put in at the end of the raft trip. A thirty-minute flight in your Jetcopter just gave you a bird's-eye view of what will take you five days to navigate when you're in your raft.

By now you may be asking, "What does a helicopter flight and raft trip have to do with building a great ministry team?"

Lots, as you'll discover. For as you turn the page, you'll be starting River School, where you come to learn important information your team needs to know to stay safe and dry on the journey. In River School you'll learn about four predictable transitions, or rapids, that every ministry team will face.

Chapter Three
River School

BEING PART OF A MINISTRY TEAM is a lot like white-water rafting, and there's perhaps no better place to hit the water than in our home state of Arizona. As the snow melts in the Rocky Mountains, the swelling streams rush down to form the Colorado River. At one point in its journey from the mountains to the ocean, the Colorado River passes through the incredibly beautiful Grand Canyon.

In some places during your raft trip, cliff walls alongside the riverbank will stretch straight up one mile from the floor to the rim of the canyon. And while snow and pine trees may lie at the top of the canyon, temperatures may reach 117 degrees alongside the river!

On your 5-day white-water trip with your ministry team, you'll navigate a section of the mighty Colorado which runs 279 miles, dropping more than two thousand feet, from Lee's Ferry to Lake Mead. And while some river runners wait for ten to twelve years for a private permit to take the ride of a lifetime, your ministry team is first in line. In fact, your vans are just pulling up to the small building you saw near the rafts when you took your helicopter tour!

GOING TO RIVER SCHOOL

We realize that for many of you reading this book, your ministry team service didn't begin with everyone going through an intense time of training like River School. For most people in ministry, joining a team meant jumping (or being tossed) into the water and swimming over to an already floating raft! Perhaps you're shooting the rapids right now as a team and hanging on for dear life. But regardless of whether you're a new team that is eager to get off to a great start or you've been teamed up for years and want to increase effectiveness and closeness, it's crucial to pull your raft out of the water long enough go through River School. *That's because River School will highlight five key insights that will become as crucial to you and your team in facing the rapids as your life preserver and paddle.*

With that in mind, let's all walk inside the small, thankfully air-conditioned, building that will be our classroom. As you grab a seat in one of the plastic folding chairs, up front your river guide is busy writing on the large whiteboard.

LIKE FATHER, LIKE SON

Your guide introduces himself as Scott Carter. He is the son of John Carter, one of the most experienced and well-known guides ever to work the Colorado.

"My father ran this river for twenty-five years and learned more than most about the ways of the river. I got to work with him for three years before he retired. Over more than two decades my father not only learned about the river, but he learned a lot about the people in his rafts. My father had an incredible way of helping people to understand how to use their God-given strengths to successfully navigate the rapids. He also had an incredible ability to use the strengths of others to compensate for any weaknesses he had on his teams. He did his best to pass this wisdom on to me, and I've been amazed to see these truths lived out daily in my raft."

FOUR PHRASES THAT HIGHLIGHT FOUR TRANSITIONS EVERY TEAM WILL FACE

On the whiteboard, Scott wrote four phrases that held the keys to successfully navigating four major *transitions,* river guide talk for "huge rapids." Scott explained as the first phrase went up on the board:

Problems and Challenges

"My father always told me that, on the river, how you approach problems and challenges in your raft is a key to staying dry and safe as a team. From setting up before you shoot the rapids to finishing strong, some in your raft will have a natural tendency to solve a problem or accept a challenge aggressively, while others see the problem or challenge and take a more passive approach. As you'll learn on the river, both styles are needed in the raft—at times digging in and challenging the river and at times having the patience to wait and ride with the current—to successfully navigate the rapids."

Then came another phrase on the board and another principle to understand:

People and Information

"One thing is for sure—it takes a team of people to navigate the rapids. Some of you will have a natural tendency to trust others in the raft, and the information you receive from them, implicitly. Others in the raft question people and information much more closely; they need to verify the information given to them before they can trust what is presented.

On the river we can make some decisions in advance. However, as my father said, 'Some decisions have to be made now, or your rafters go swimming.' Our ability to strike this delicate balance will determine whether we build a strong bond of trust or breed mistrust as we travel down the river."

A third phrase then went up on the whiteboard:

Pace and Change

"Something that's true on the river is absolutely true in teams and relationships: change is inevitable. My father encouraged me to watch closely how people on my team handled change because it is one of the most critical factors in safely running the rapids. In particular, some people are going to love it when things change and naturally move _faster_ in the face of increased pressure. These people look forward to unexpected circumstances on the river and will react quickly when needed. Other people will have a natural, God-given bent to slow down and systematically approach the changes ahead. They are good at planning ahead for such changes, but unexpected change is difficult for them, and their reaction time is slower. We need to take advantage of both styles at different times on the river."

And then came a fourth phrase you must learn if you are to succeed on the river:

Rules and Procedures

"The National Park Service has produced a manual that outlines the rules and procedures to be followed while white-water rafting on the Colorado. Every person who rafts on the river is required to sign a waiver stating that he or she has read the manual and agrees to follow it.

"My father taught me that the manual will give some rafters great comfort because they follow rules instinctively and, especially on the river, feel that the rules keep them safe. Others view the manual as a list of suggestions. They have no problem breaking the rules, especially if they see good reason to do so. This difference can cause more conflict between rafters than anything else. My father knew that managing this conflict between the rule-followers and rule-breakers was crucial to a safe and fun trip."

A FINAL PHRASE

With this, Scott wrote his father's most famous saying on the board:

> Every river,
> Every raft,
> and every person
> is different.
> Your unique strengths
> are the very things your
> team needs to run the
> rapids successfully.
> —John Carter,
>   river guide

"I hope you enjoyed River School. My father wrote the quote I just gave you early in his career. He guided rafts on the Colorado for twenty-five years, and he swears that every day was different. I believe what my father wrote. I'll need to call on the unique strengths in each of you before our trip is over, so be prepared."

Scott shows you where the dining hall is and sits down to eat with you. After dinner he suggests that everyone get acquainted with their sleeping bag. The raft will hit the water just after sunrise the next morning. As your team prepares to leave, Scott adds, "For your reading pleasure tonight, I want to give you something that's special to me. I have a copy of my father's diary for each of you. Actually, it's the diary of his last rafting trip as a guide. Since most of you will be up anyway, thinking about our trip, read this before you go to bed. Let it sink in. If you're like most of my other rafters, you'll learn as much from my father's experiences as you did at River School.

"See you in the morning."

Chapter Four
The "Problems and Challenges" Transition

RIVER GUIDE'S DIARY: DAY ONE

*OUR FIRST DAY OUT proved to be a great day on the river.
Everyone arrived at the launch site on time and with everything in order. As our base-camp team strapped our camping
equipment and food into the raft, it was clear that everyone
was filled with excitement and anticipation. While the final
details for our trip were being attended to, I pulled the team
aside to give them some last-minute instructions.*

*The sun was just starting to warm up the morning air as
we gathered. The release of thousands of gallons of ice-cold
water from the bottom of Glen Canyon Dam upstream had
already raised the level of the river from the day before. The
team had been briefed last night about the hazards we might
face in the next few days. Everyone had signed the necessary
disclosure and liability papers. This then was really their
first opportunity to meet me and to ask me questions, and my
first chance to size them up. I knew from their applications
that a few had been white-water rafting before, but no one
had been on anything like the mighty Colorado.*

*To instill some confidence, I started off by telling them
that this would be my twenty-fifth season guiding rafts
through the Grand Canyon and that no one had ever been*

seriously injured on my watch. That's not to say we hadn't
had a few scary times when people ended up in the water.
What I didn't tell them was that this was my last trip. I would
be officially retired as soon as we finished. Then I told them
about the day ahead.

"Today, we are launching out on what will be a life-changing experience for you all," I said. "There is no place on earth
like what you are going to see and experience over the next few
days, and I'm looking forward to guiding you through it all."

I told them that the first part of our trip would be smooth,
but then we would come to our first major obstacle—Haystack
Rock. From positioning in the raft to previewing how each
person might handle a problem that came up, I needed to know
something about each rafter. I began by asking each person
why he or she had come on the trip. As usual, about half came
to challenge the river. I assigned them seats in the front of the
raft that first day. I would need their aggressiveness to successfully set up for Haystack Rock. The others had come to relax
and unwind or simply to enjoy some great scenery. I instructed
them to sit in the back of the raft as we began. While they
didn't realize it, I knew we would need their steadiness in the
second stage of setting up for the rapids of Haystack Rock.

On this first day, in order to keep everyone high and dry,
we were going to first set up for Haystack Rock by paddling as
hard as we could. With everyone digging into the river as
things got louder and we neared these first rapids, I would
maneuver us so that the back end of our boat would literally
bump up against a particular spot on Haystack Rock. At that
point, rather than continuing to dig in with our paddles,
everyone—especially those in the front of the raft—would
need to pull their paddles in. This would leave us right in line
with the current, which would take us straight through the rest
of the rapids safely. I stressed to my team that once we bumped
the rock, if people didn't stop paddling, we would end up getting turned around and stuck in the hydraulics, or worse. And
"worse" could easily mean being turned sideways and all of us
going swimming.

Having given my morning instructions and with everything prepared for our trip, we all got into the raft and set out

from Lee's Ferry. There weren't any serious challenges for the first few hours on the river. The water was running fairly fast, it was a good time for people to get familiar with the feel of the raft and their paddle, and time went by quickly. After a nice shore lunch, we headed straight for Haystack Rock. A nervous excitement filled the air, and I reminded the team to listen carefully to my instructions.

We made a good approach, but we started to slide a little left. Everyone was digging in, but several rafters on the right side were leaning in toward the middle of the boat to avoid the white water. I shouted that everyone needed to lean toward the outside and paddle hard. With that, everyone hunkered down and dug in. That set us up just right. About two seconds before we hit the rock, I called "oars in." We hit the rock where we needed to, the current picked us up immediately, and we were off to the races! A couple of seconds later, two of my river-eaters up front decided we weren't going fast enough and started to paddle. I had to shout "oars in" several times. Fortunately for all of us, they listened. For the next three minutes, we had a great ride through the rapids.

After a wonderful dinner and an even better sunset, I told the team that we needed to get to bed to make sure we were ready for the adventures we would face tomorrow. Devil's Den lay ahead. I wouldn't know until the morning how high the water would be running. We all went to bed, and I'm sure that I wasn't the only one who stayed awake for a bit to gaze up at the incredible array of stars that danced above us in the moonless sky. I would sure miss this sight.

What do the challenges of Haystack Rock have to do with your ministry? The first unavoidable set of rapids that every team will face is learning how to handle problems and challenges, some as big and demanding as Haystack Rock. Just like the team on the raft, each member of a ministry team approaches problems or challenges in a different way.

Some naturally take an aggressive approach and charge right into issues, while others take a much more passive approach. Some want to paddle hard, competing against the river from the moment they push off, while some people just want to let the current take them along. Each approach can be right in a given circumstance. Aggressive problem-solving and more passive problem-solving can both be strengths. If you're aware of the natural tension that can come from working closely with people very different from you, your team can capitalize on each of these strengths. The question, then, facing your ministry team is, do you know who is in the raft with you and how they naturally handle problems and challenges?

Let's share an example of how not factoring in a person's natural problem-solving bent proved extremely costly to one church.

Several years ago, there was a three-year-old church plant that was seeing tremendous ministry gains but was stretched thin financially. As attendance continued to grow, the church quickly reached the maximum capacity of the school auditorium where they met weekly. It was clear to everyone that the church leadership had to find a new facility. After much prayer, the church leaders decided to take the major step of looking for their own property to build on. The problem these elders faced was that property in the growth area where they wanted to locate was simply out of their price range.

After much deliberation, the church leadership appointed one of the elders, Ed, a successful businessman, to look for property in the area. One of the benefits of choosing Ed was that he was a lifelong resident of the area. He had seen the town grow up over the past fifty years, and he knew most of the original families that had settled the farmland that was now a thriving city. Only a few days later, a friend tipped Ed off that an old farmer they both knew was open to selling twenty-five acres of property near one of the major highways. That afternoon Ed scheduled a meeting with the farmer.

The two drove over to the property, and Ed liked what he saw. When the farmer told him the price, Ed immediately knew the farmer, a Christian, was offering the church a tremendous deal.

That's when Ed grabbed his paddle, dug in with all his might, and made an offer on the spot for the property. To secure the land until they could draw up a formal contract, Ed gave the farmer a check for $50,000 in earnest money from his business account.

Ed knew the building fund had enough money to cover his commitment, and he could get a check from the church that night when he delivered the good news to his fellow elders. So he called an emergency meeting of the board for that same evening.

Once they all had arrived, Ed was able to share the good news that God had answered their prayers; their search for property was over! Their overcrowding problems were solved. They were now the owners of an incredible piece of property that would be their new church home! There was as much shock as excitement in the room as Ed continued with his sudden announcement, but then came a devastating blow. As Ed told the elders where the land was, one of the men present remembered looking at the same property six months earlier.

"Ed," the man interrupted, "I looked at that property. Did you know, or did the farmer tell you, that the zoning commission has put an indefinite hold on zoning that land for anything other than a farm?" There was dead silence in the room. "And Ed, a friend of mine at city hall told me that even if the land was rezoned, it was going to cost someone at least another $1 million to get city utilities to the property. Did something change?"

Ed's heart sank. He hadn't asked about the restrictions on the land. And he hadn't told them yet that he had already committed the church by writing a check! It suddenly hit Ed that if they were to pull out of the deal, he might lose part or all of the $50,000 he had put up on the church's behalf and be in huge trouble with his company!

There are times when aggressive problem-solving is the best thing to do, and people with this naturally aggressive tendency are the right ones for the job. But by signing the contract and committing the church's (and actually his company's money), Ed had overstepped his authority.

At times, acting quickly, and with limited information, can create an even bigger problem then the original one! This is why understanding who is on your team and how they deal with problems and challenges is so important. Not taking the time or effort to find out who the Lord has placed on your team is a great way to create more problems than you solve. It may mean your team misses important opportunities. It may mean your team moves forward when it shouldn't have. It may mean problems facing your team become worse than they already are. It may mean internal conflict among your team members.

Strengths and Limitations

Now is a good time to ask, "Just who is in our raft when it comes to facing problems and challenges?" Keep in mind the three core principles we introduced in chapter 2:

1. Understanding your own God-given strengths.
2. Recognizing and respecting the God-given strengths of those you work *with*.
3. Blending differences among team members.

Certainly, the dramatic example of Ed is a case where someone pushed his God-given strengths to an extreme. But don't misunderstand the example above. It is important to have people in your raft who are willing to dig in and solve problems, but these same people also need to know when to pull their paddle out of the water.

To help you see and better understand the strengths and limitations of people with natural, aggressive problem-solving bents, as well as people who approach problems more passively, below are two important tables. These tables also include descriptors that show how the strengths of each style, when pushed to an extreme, can cause conflict with other team members.

		STRENGTHS		
A	Daring	Competitive	Forceful	Determined
G	Self-Starter	Tenacious	Forward-Looking	
G				
R		**POTENTIAL LIMITATIONS**		
E	Impatient	Domineering	Blunt	Risktaker
S	Strong-Willed	Egotistical	Desires Power	
S				
I	**POTENTIAL SOURCES OF CONFLICT WITH OTHERS**			
V		Intimidating	Confrontational	
E		Close-Minded	Defensive	

People with an aggressive problem-solving style have many traits that are valuable to a team. They are results oriented. They will get the job done if given the appropriate authority. No one needs to push them. They naturally have a drive to make things happen. Problems and challenges are opportunities rather than reasons to quit. In fact, people with this style crave a challenge. Without one they will become bored, and their motivation will disappear. Often people with this trait will manifest their aggressive tendency by direct questioning of others. They don't mess around!

It is clear to see how these strengths could energize a team. People with these strengths can move a team forward simply by the force of their will. When pushed to an extreme, however, these same strengths can become limitations and sources of conflict on the team. If people with this style are not careful, their strengths of being competitive, forceful, and determined can quickly become domineering, egotistical, and impatient. These limitations can lead to open conflict that can plague a ministry team.

For people with an aggressive style, that conflict might arise most frequently with another person who has an aggressive style. It isn't easy for two strong-willed, forceful people to work together, especially when they have differing opinions on what to do or how to do it.

This style can also clash with the more passive style. Team members with an aggressive style can easily overwhelm those with a passive style. The more passive team members experience the person with the aggressive style as intimidating and confrontational. The more passive team members then have the option to either fight back, escalating the conflict, or to back off and let the aggressive person run the show. The latter can lead to bad decision-making when the more thoughtful, cautious person is silenced. For instance, when someone with an aggressive style is questioned about his or her handling of a situation, that person can often perceive the questioning as a personal attack. But the reality is that someone operating with a more passive style is simply being cautious to ensure that no important details are being overlooked. When that aggressive person responds with a counterattack, the recipient will feel as if his opinion isn't important to the process and will normally retreat.

The aggressive style asks questions and demands answers, often without feeling the need for tact or diplomacy. The person with the passive style may give in, and the person with the aggressive style may believe he has won over the passive team member. Many times, however, the person with the passive style has simply retreated to avoid conflict.

STRENGTHS

P
A
S
S
I
V
E

Conservative   Low-Key   Careful   Prepared
Considerate   Vigilant   Self-Control

POTENTIAL LIMITATIONS

Avoids Conflict   Disagreeable
Slow Decision Making   Afraid   Passive

SOURCES OF CONFLICT WITH OTHERS

Obstacle to Progress   Close-Minded   Indecisive
Lack of Creativity   Refusing to Confront   Unmotivated

People who are passive when confronting problems and challenges are valuable to any ministry team. By nature they are conservative and cautious. They want to know all the facts before they move forward to solve a problem or challenge. The Boy Scout motto, "Be Prepared," could be their motto too.

Vigilance is an important trait for the person with the passive style. People with this style are like sentries at the castle gate, constantly on the lookout for the best interests of the team.

The passive style can be critical for a team to have when difficult decisions must be made or complex problems arise. Typically, these decisions can't be made and these problems addressed as effectively with an aggressive style. The person with a passive style will insist on studying the problem before a solution is sought. Decisions are purposefully and carefully considered. No hasty decisions will be made if the passive style is in charge.

The greatest strength of those with the passive style can also be their biggest limitation. Decisions are sometimes made so slowly that the opportunity is lost. People with a passive style can be too conservative and careful. If consensus is necessary quickly, people with a passive style may not be able to respond. Decisions may not be made in a timely manner. The forward motion of the team can grind to a halt and the passive person can appear to be closed-minded.

People on the same team with different styles of being aggressive or passive need to remember the goals of the team. Knowing they have naturally different ways of trying to achieve these goals is a key insight to group closeness and effectiveness. The aggressive style wants to capture the moment and act quickly. The passive style wants to consider all the possibilities and access all important information before moving ahead.

Go through the tables above carefully, thinking closely about each person on your team. Ask yourself the following questions:

- Who on our team is naturally aggressive at problem solving?
- Who is naturally passive or cautious?
- What's an example of our team's history when this push and pull between aggressive and passive problem solving caused a problem for us?
- What's a potential problem situation we'll soon face where we could use the information in this chapter to better prepare ourselves for success?

The difference in how people react to problems and challenges is just the first of four major factors your team needs to consider to successfully navigate the waters ahead. The second key factor surfaced on day two of running the rapids.

Chapter Five
The "People and Information" Transition

★

RIVER GUIDE'S DIARY: DAY TWO

ONE OF THE HARDEST LESSONS *to learn as a white-water guide is that your reputation is built as much on what you don't do on the river as on what you do. Today was a great reminder of that principle for me.*

I knew the flow from the water released from Glen Canyon Dam yesterday had probably run through the canyon. That meant I was going to have to watch the water levels as we came up on Devil's Den. The rapids there are caused when the Little Colorado rushes into the larger Colorado River. Even when the water is going fast through the rapids, the water is not always deep enough to make it through without tearing up a raft on the rocks. I told the team that we might have to keep our options open about riding the rapids or putting in to shore and walking the raft downstream to avoid the rocks. I'd have to scout out that section on our approach to know what we were going to do.

Before we got to Devil's Den, the slow-moving water we traveled on meant that we had to paddle for most of the early going. We were also able to run some nice rapids before we put in for lunch. As we sat around eating our sandwiches, I could tell everyone was already tired from the long haul upstream.

When we finally drifted close to Devil's Den, everyone was beat from all the paddling. I kept checking the water levels along the canyon wall to see how we might fare if we tried to push through the rapids. We could see the mouth of the Little Colorado coming in from the side, which is a beautiful sight. Everyone was talking as we came around the bend, and I got my first look at the rapids.

The first thing that concerned me was that the white water was running across the whole river. That meant two things: first, that the water was running low; second, there wasn't a clear channel of deep water that we could use to make a run through the rapids. As we got closer, I saw the larger rocks sticking out further downstream, plus some nasty holes and hydraulics showing themselves. I wasn't looking forward to our having to lug the boat downstream, even a quarter-mile, but I knew the danger that we could be facing if we tried to shoot the rapids.

I broke the bad news to the team, and everyone in the raft started paddling towards shore. The paddlers up front were grumbling because they still wanted to shoot the rapids, but as we put to shore, I reminded everyone there was a reason this was called Devil's Den.

The grumbling in the boat escalated into an argument when we hit dry land. Some of the rafters from the front of the raft quickly inspected the rapids and were insistent that we push back out and take on the rapids. Thankfully, the majority was intent on following my lead and wanted to start carrying the raft to the place we could reenter the river. I ended the argument by telling the team we were not going to run Devil's Den. We would rest for a few minutes and take the raft downstream. I told the guys up front that they were trusting what they could see in the rapids, but the danger lay in what they couldn't see beneath the water. While the response from the up front rafters was inspiring and enthusiastic, it was ill-advised.

It only took a few minutes for them to find out why. As we stretched out on the riverbank to rest before heading downriver, another raft came by. I recognized the guide, who was a notorious young hotshot that had a couple of his crews busted up last summer. I saw that they were going to try and shoot the

rapids. I called out to him that the rocks looked bad. He
shouted back that they would be fine. I could see my river-
eaters giving me the eye.

As the raft hit the first part of the rapids, the front of the
boat bucked up and dumped the two rafters up front into the
water. Everyone else in the raft was scrambling to get them in.
One of them hit a rock pretty hard, but his helmet saved him
from serious injury. The other one climbed up on a rock and sat
down as the raft went by. The river had them now because no
one was paddling. They got turned sideways, and the guide
didn't see the big rock in the middle of the river until it was too
late. They hit the rock sideways, and the raft flipped straight
up on its right side. Everyone went into the drink.

We all went into action. We grabbed our rescue lines and
started running down the river. We finally got lines out to
them and pulled them in. Three of them had some nasty cuts
and bruises, but the rest were all right.

Once we made sure they were OK and base camp had been
contacted to come and get them, we walked our raft downstream and got back in. We took it nice and slow for about
another hour. Fortunately, there weren't any more rapids
before we pulled in to camp for the night. Once we set up our
tents and put dinner on to cook, we had a chance to talk as we
gathered around the campfire. My river-eaters sheepishly
apologized for not trusting my judgment.

As we all sat there, recounting what had happened to the
other team, I told them that they should learn some lessons from
our experience today. No matter how optimistic the team may
be about taking on the rapids, they couldn't trust their own intu-
ition or abilities; they had to trust what I knew about the river.

We have another rough day tomorrow, with a number of
difficult rapids downstream, including Upset Rapids. I think
the team trusts me now more than they did this morning, but
tomorrow will require doing things differently and making
some changes, and I hope they can adjust. If so, we'll have
a great time on the river tomorrow.

Our team of rafters learned a valuable lesson about trust at
Devil's Den, which provides us a great opportunity to discuss how

the next transition could play out in the context of your ministry team. The next unavoidable rapid your ministry team will face involves *people and information—namely, how your team members trust others and the information they receive from them.* Are your team members trusting of information they receive from others, or do they look at information they receive with a more skeptical eye? Do they view what others say using logic and facts, or are they influenced by words that stir their emotions?

How trusting or skeptical the people are that make up your group is a critical issue for building an outstanding team. For example, how many people on your team would you say are naturally optimistic and believe the best about everyone and every circumstance? People like this usually need to be with others and have a high need to be accepted by them. Highly relational people tend to be trusting. For them, trust is an emotional issue. Unfortunately, trust for them can be indiscriminate, and they can be taken advantage of easily.

Maybe you would say that most of your team members tend to be more realistic and skeptical. People with this style want the facts and figures. You need to give them proof before they will trust you, even if you have shown yourself to be a reliable source of information in the past. Their skeptical nature can lead to its own problems in a ministry team setting.

How you and your team members try to influence others is just as important. Generally, you will attempt to influence others in the same way you are influenced by others. The optimist will use lots of words to elicit emotion, as well as the force of their personality, to influence others. On the other hand, the realist will present facts and figures delivered within a system of well-reasoned logic to be persuasive. What style do you use to influence others on your team? How do they react to your style, and what does that say about them?

As we discussed in chapter 4, there are two equally sound approaches to problem solving: an aggressive and a passive approach. Both have strengths and limitations. When the two approaches clash on a ministry team, the conflict is often inevitable and predictable. *This is certainly true for the People and Information Transition as well.* Typically, within every team there are people with two distinct ways of influencing, and being influenced, by others: an optimistic/emotional approach and a realistic/fact-based approach. Both styles are needed on the team in different circumstances. The conflict between the styles is predictable but can be reduced or eliminated if team members understand their strengths and limitations and the strengths and limitations of others and are committed to blending them to make the team better.

In our work with various ministry teams, we have seen the conflict surrounding the People and Information Transition stretch teams to the breaking point.

Take, for instance, a phone call we received from the board of directors of a large parachurch ministry. Jack, the CEO, was a visionary type who excelled at presenting and selling the ministry's vision to donors. Clay, the CFO, was the consummate accountant and was dedicated to making sure the numbers reflected the true financial situation of the organization at all times. With the recent economic downturn, the ministry began to see a steady decline in donations. This trend was compounded by Jack's reluctance to communicate the financial needs of the ministry to donors.

While Jack was recognized as an up-and-coming evangelical leader and was being invited to speak at Christian conferences and conventions, the ministry was slipping into a serious financial problem. Clay reported the downward spiral to Jack on a weekly basis. He prepared reports with bar graphs and all the facts and figures to document the monthly shortfalls. Jack read the reports, but he refused to let the facts get in the way of communicating his optimistic vision for the ministry. He knew that the ministry had seen rough times before and believed that donations were certain to pick up.

However, when the situation continued for more than six months, Clay made plans to lay off several members of the support staff. Jack strongly disagreed with such a move. He made his feelings abundantly clear by delivering a lengthy tirade during a staff meeting about being committed to the ministry and having faith in God. His words were clearly directed at Clay, and everyone knew it.

As finances continued to worsen and Jack refused to acknowledge the dire straits the ministry was facing, Clay felt that he had to take the matter directly to the board of directors. We were asked by the board to become involved to help assess the situation.

Clay and Jack both took the Leading From Your Strengths® assessment, the same assessment you will have the opportunity to take after reading chapter 8. After we reviewed their reports and discussed their unique, God-given strengths with them, it quickly became clear that *trust* was the critical issue in the relational strain between the two. Jack was an excellent communicator, and he relied heavily on his relational skills to sell the ministry's vision. He was an extreme optimist and used words filled with emotion to influence others. It wasn't surprising to find out that Clay communicated primarily through logic and data. He was a realist who prided himself in being precise and accurate. The conflict between the two was predictable. Unfortunately, things deteriorated rapidly because of the financial woes of the ministry.

As we discussed the situation further with these two men, we discovered that when Clay came to Jack about the finances and asked critical questions based on the information in his spread-sheets and bar graphs, Clay was speaking a language that Jack didn't respond to. Jack took Clay's detailed reports as an attack on his ability to run the ministry and felt that Clay didn't trust him to connect with donors anymore. Likewise, Clay did not respond well to Jack's emotional outbursts, which made him feel as if Jack was condemning him for doing his job, but even worse, for a lack of faith in God.

We then discussed the different styles of communicating and how people with these styles influence and are influenced by others. Jack was able to see that Clay had enormous respect for him and believed that he was the right man to get the ministry back on track. Clay was finally able to express that degree of trust in a relational manner. In turn, Jack was able to see that it was Clay's job to give him accurate financial information, even if it was bad news. Clay's critical evaluation of the financial data wasn't a questioning of Jack's executive decision-making abilities. Jack realized the reports Clay gave him painted an accurate picture of the ministry's finances and that he should trust them. Once Jack and Clay understood their unique strengths and how to blend those strengths to become a more effective team, they were able to attack the financial problem rather than each other.

Three weeks after meeting with Jack and Clay, we received a phone call to update us on the ministry's progress. Several of their largest donors, many of whom had not been aware of the dire financial needs, expressed their continued support for the ministry through significant gifts. This energized Jack, who began to actively communicate the ministry's vision but also the need for resources to accomplish their goals. Clay worked closely with Jack to provide this information for Jack's presentations. They became more of a team than ever before. The conflict between Jack and Clay, which had been as much a threat to the organization as its financial troubles, had been all but eliminated through a common understanding of their different strengths and a commitment to blend them for the good of the team.

STRENGTHS AND LIMITATIONS

The People and Information Transition revolves around whether we trust other people and the information they give us, as well as how we influence others when we provide information to them. Do we rely on emotional communication, or do we use facts and data to influence others? Are we influenced by others who approach us relationally or more analytically? These two styles are different, but both need to be understood if team members are going to communicate with one another effectively.

Let's go back and look at the three core principles listed in chapter 2:

1. Understanding your own God-given strengths.
2. Recognizing and respecting the God-given strengths of those you work *with*.
3. Blending differences among team members.

How do your team members influence others on the team? What is the best way to influence them? These are critical factors in the effectiveness of any team. Knowing this about yourself and the others on your team can be invaluable. This knowledge gives the team the ability to empower its members to lead from their strengths.

The following tables list the strengths and potential limitations of the different styles in the People and Information

Transition, as well as the predictable areas of conflict that could arise when these styles clash.

O P T I M I S T	**STRENGTHS** Optimistic Inspiring Friendly Outgoing Enthusiastic Creative Negotiates Conflict **POTENTIAL LIMITATIONS** Trusts Indiscriminately Lack of Discernment Impulsive Inattentive to Details Overconfident Unrealistic **POTENTIAL SOURCES OF CONFLICT WITH OTHERS** Unreliable Overestimates Abilities Overcommits Poor Listener Unrestrained Talks Too Much

Optimists are expressive, outgoing individuals with a high need for social interaction. They are parties waiting to happen! They love to talk and communicate in an emotional, enthusiastic way, which makes them eager to share their feelings with others! They instinctively believe the best about people and trust what people tell them. Optimists can be creative problem-solvers, often using their innate persuasive ability to influence others to their point of view. These strengths make the optimist an invaluable, fun part of any ministry team.

One of an optimist's greatest strengths is their ability to influence others. Unfortunately, they can also be easily influenced *by* others. Optimists tend to trust indiscriminately, making them vulnerable to being taken advantage of, which can lead the team in the wrong direction. Because they are optimistic and believe they can "do it all," they have a hard time saying no to anyone or anything. This can sometimes cause others to think of the optimist as naïve or even reckless. This can also lead to the optimist's avoiding conflict, especially when it involves difficult issues having to do with people. In short, optimists are not naturally effective when reprimanding and disciplining people. Another source of conflict with optimists is their penchant for fun and talking, which can cause problems when it is time for the team to get serious.

While the optimist has many strengths, those strengths, pushed to an extreme, can become liabilities. Their optimism leads to overpromising that can cause optimists to underdeliver. Others can see optimists as unreliable and may voice this when it is crunch time.

Because optimists trust so completely, they may not always have accurate perceptions of others. For example, someone who is working on or with the team may have proven himself untrustworthy or undependable on several occasions. When it comes time to trust that person again, the optimist may remain steadfast in the belief that the person will act trustworthy *this time*. This can generate conflict with others on the team who feel the person has shown his or her true colors, and it is time to move on. Once it is identified, the conflict between the optimist and others is usually resolved quickly, thanks to the natural tendency for the optimist to be a peacemaker.

	STRENGTHS		
R	Realistic	Good Listener	Calm	Factual
E	Reflective	Critical Thinker	Logical	
A				
L	**POTENTIAL LIMITATIONS**		
I	Critical of Others	Over Analytical	Introspective
S	Nonemotional	Pessimistic	
T	**POTENTIAL SOURCES OF CONFLICT WITH OTHERS**		
	Unfriendly	Withdrawn	Self-Absorbed
	Skeptical	Uncommunicative	Distrusting

The realist has many strengths as well. Realists are logical and critical thinkers. They are not easily taken advantage of. If you have a difficult decision or complex issue, the realist is the one you want to help think it through. Although realists tend to form fewer friendships than do optimists, those friendships are generally deeper. Realists are good listeners, which may be one reason for those strong relationships.

One reason realists tend to form fewer friendships is that they can be difficult to get to know. They can be seen as unemotional. It may be hard to know how they feel about a certain issue. The realist's skeptical nature can result in others viewing them as overly critical. In some cases this skeptical or questioning nature can cause people to look at the realist as pessimistic.

One of the main ways this natural bent of the realist causes conflict with others is by communicating distrust. When realists question optimists, they are simply asking for information they believe necessary in order to make the right decision. This questioning often communicates to the optimist that the realist doesn't trust him.

Another source of conflict for realists is a perception by others that they are not friendly. The unemotinoal demeanor of the realist, which is frequently difficult to read, can cause this reaction. In some cases, the realist can be viewed as withdrawn or a loner. All of this presents the potential for serious conflict in a team environment.

The conflict these differing styles cause is inevitable, very *predictable*. Knowing this and acting upon it in advance can help the team achieve greater heights than it ever could have by leaving the conflict unaddressed. If the members of your team make the effort to adapt their communication with other team members who have a different style, effective communication will increase, and the team will flourish.

Review the tables and consider which style your team members might be. Ask yourself these questions:

- Are you naturally trusting of people and information, or are you more skeptical?
- How about your fellow team members?
- In what ways have you seen the contrast between the optimist and the realist affect your team?
- How can you and your other team members use the information in this chapter to make the team better?

It's time now to look at Day Three, and another crucial "Transition" every team must face.

Chapter Six
The "Pace and Change" Transition

★

RIVER GUIDE'S DIARY: DAY THREE

AFTER STRIKING CAMP THIS MORNING, *I took some time to discuss the day ahead with my team. I explained that the river was running high because of another release from Glen Canyon Dam and how that might change the way we approached the river. It would be a transitional day all around. We were going to see some dramatic geological changes. The Colorado River was digging deeper into the earth and exposing layers of rock almost a mile into the ground. But the new geology was going to change the nature of the river as well.*

The most difficult spot for us would be Upset Rapids at the end of the day. When the water runs high, it creates a whirlpool effect that requires a unique setup: going in backward. If you hit it just right, the whirlpool will shoot you out of the whirlpool with the raft pointed downriver. If you don't, anything can happen.

About an hour after we set out, we hit our first long stretch of calmer river, so I encouraged everyone to hop out and float. Everyone in the front of the boat bailed out quickly. With their life vests on, if they kept their feet up and away from the rocks on the bottom, they could ride along with the flow of the river. I convinced all but two rafters to try it. The two that wouldn't go looked at me as if I was out of my mind.

To them, jumping out of a perfectly good raft into cold, fast-flowing water with rapids up ahead was not their idea of a good time. I made sure to remind them that before the day was out they might be taking an involuntary swim anyway.

After stopping for lunch, I told the team that we were about to hit a number of serious rapids downriver, including Upset Rapids, and I would have to change the seating in the raft to prepare for it. The rafters in front would be changing seats with the rafters in the back of the raft. Predictably, some members of both groups howled in protest. Most of them took it in stride. One thing was certain, all of them would have to change the way they approached the river.

As we came up on our first serious rapids of the day, I could see that my new front four were a little scared. I told everybody to dig in, and we attacked the first major wave that almost sent us vertical. I could hear the screams up front just as we hit another ugly wave. Everyone's adrenaline was pumping by the time we got through the rapids. I told them that we had another set of rapids coming up, and everyone shouted enthusiastically, especially in the front of the raft. Apparently the change was growing on them!

The excitement died when we came around the next bend. Sitting right in the middle of the river was a monster hole. I had never seen one here before, and we were too close to get around it. We needed to get some more weight up toward the front of the boat, or we were going to flip. I shouted to the two river-eaters right in front of me to move to the front of the raft, kneel down, and hold on. We only had about ten seconds to make the change before we hit the hole, so I encouraged them to move fast. One of the ladies up front turned around and screamed at me to tell her what was going to happen. I shrugged. The thrill of the last rapids had become full-fledged panic.

We hit the hole dead-on. The river towered at least ten feet over the raft as we went down. We shot up and would have flipped over backward, but the extra weight up front saved us. We came crashing down, and we all got wet, but no one went overboard. The two guys who moved to the front were now lying in six inches of water. We sent up a cheer for them as they headed to the back of the raft.

*We ran the next two sets of rapids with no problems. It had
been a great day so far, but Upset Rapids was ahead of us. You
can see Upset Rapids from way upstream, which gives you
plenty of time to set up and make any changes you need to
make. If you're lucky, you can watch someone else go in before
you, but when we got there, we were the only ones in sight.
Thankfully, these rapids looked just like I thought they would.*

*As we were setting up to turn the raft and go backward
through the rapids, several rafters wondered out loud if this
would work. I assured them I had done this successfully before.
I couldn't help but add, "But you never know, so hold on tight!"*

*As we hit the whirlpool at Upset Rapids, the nose of the
raft lifted up, raising some shrill screams from up front. It
was just like the first hill on a roller coaster. Seconds later
the whirlpool turned us and spit us out, and we shot forward
into the rest of the rapids. I told everyone to dig in. We were
shooting the rapids awfully fast, but it was awesome!
Everyone was hooting and hollering as we finished up the
moment.*

*By the time we pulled into camp for the night, everyone
said that this had been the best day yet. They didn't know that
the Great Divide was waiting for them tomorrow, and I didn't
tell them. I didn't want to spoil the moment.*

Change can have a great impact on your team. Change is
a constant for ministry teams and is the third inevitable rapid
that all ministry teams must deal with. Sometimes change appears
abruptly; other times it approaches with fair warning. *How your
team members react to change is critical to the success of the team.*
Do your team members take change in stride, adjusting on the fly
to different circumstances, or do they need preparation before
change and logical reasons to do so?

As we saw with the prior transitions of problem-solving
(passive or aggressive) and influence (optimist or realist), change
is something we all have to face. However, the approaches we take
can be radically different. When change arises within teams, some
team members are going to want to know the purpose behind the
changes and want to understand what direction the team will be
going once the change has been made. Time to consider the change

is a critical part of their acceptance of it because they are looking for assurance that change is meaningful and beneficial. These team members are more slow paced, loyal, steadfast, deliberate, and systematic. In rough waters they are a source of stability, calm, and patience.

Other members of your team will adapt to change quickly and will not need to have the reasons for change explained to them. They are not looking for predictability because they are alert to opportunities that arise suddenly, and they want to seize them. The uncharted waters of change provide them the chance to use their strengths of flexibility and resilience. These team members may get restless when operating at a steady pace. But they can bring a dynamic intensity to a project that can energize a team to go further and do more than it otherwise would.

Both of these approaches to change are ingredients for a stable yet progressive team. Harnessing the push and pull of change can drive your team forward to accomplish its goals. But conflicts can easily develop over these two approaches. A slow, methodical pace may not be satisfying to someone wanting a faster pace. A systematic worker who gets in an established groove and prefers to stay there will clash with someone who has a more wide-open, innovative bent. When these two styles collide, slower paced team members may stand their ground and resist change just for the sake of resisting. The change agent may begin to question the status quo repeatedly simply to exert influence and desire for change. Both reactions can cause the progress of the team to hit a standstill. The predictability of the conflict, however, makes for a ready solution. The conflict can be reduced or eliminated if team members know how they react to change and how others on the team will react. When change arises, the strengths of each team member can be used to ensure that the required change accomplishes the goals of the team.

A Team Example of Embracing and Resisting Change

A situation in which we recently acted in an advisory capacity involved a conflict in a growing, vibrant church between Andrew, an ambitious, new youth pastor, and Al, the longtime church facilities manager. Andrew was hired because of his

success in attracting, discipling, and activating teens while he
was with a local youth ministry. Al, who had served the church
for more than ten years with distinction, was known for his calm
demeanor and his meticulous maintenance of the church.

One of Andrew's prime ministry opportunities was the relationships and the contacts he developed with the local high
school students at athletic events. He would gather a group to go
to a nearby fast-food restaurant after football and basketball
games. Being teenagers, the groups were loud and boisterous, an
energy Andrew thrived on. But after bringing a large group of
students to his favorite restaurant, he was asked by the manager
not to come back.

Knowing that these times of impromptu ministry were important for connecting with the teens, he began thinking about alter-
natives. He remembered his church, which was only a couple of
miles from the high school, had a fellowship hall.

The following Friday night during the football game, he
invited students to meet at the church after the game. At half-
time, Andrew called the local pizza place and ordered twenty
pizzas to be delivered two hours later at the fellowship hall. He
left for the church right before the game to open up the facilities
and to get out the plates and cups and set up the tables and
chairs they would need. Minutes later he was delighted as kids
came streaming through the doors. He estimated that at least
seventy-five kids were there, and he was able to speak with a
number of kids he had never met before. About midnight the
last of them left. A few needed a ride home, and Andrew jumped
at the chance to spend more time with kids. Thrilled with what
happened that night, Andrew shut off the lights, locked the
doors, and left. He (for the first and last time) called the senior
pastor, Jim, on his cell phone on the way home. Jim was excited
about Andrew's success but not as excited about being called
after midnight.

When Al stopped by Saturday afternoon to make sure the
church was ready for services on Sunday morning, he was
greeted with the devastation wrought the night before. Pizza
boxes, napkins, and cups of soda littered the fellowship hall. All
of the tables were still set up, and the chairs were scattered
about the place. When Al called Jim to find out who had used

the fellowship hall, he was told about the unplanned teen meeting the night before. To say the least, Al was not happy. He reminded Jim that he was supposed to know whenever the facilities were being used and who was using them. Jim talked Al down from the ledge, telling him that as far as he knew, the gathering the night before was a one-time event. Al calmed down as he spent the next several hours cleaning up and going to the store to replace the used items. But he still wasn't happy.

Little did Al know that first thing Monday morning, Andrew was preparing a flier for the following Friday night's "Fifth Quarter" to hand out to students at the high school. The Friday night event had gone so well that Andrew decided to make it a regular event. The Wednesday after-school Bible study doubled in size that week, and it seemed that there might be even more students coming after the football game. When Friday rolled around, Andrew and the gang were back at the church, this time with thirty pizzas, which were devoured in record time. That night the gang was close to 150 students. Again, Andrew had to take a carload of kids home, so he locked up and left in a hurry.

That Saturday afternoon, Al came into the church again. This time he knew who had made the mess, so there was no need to call Jim. He was fuming as he had to spend another afternoon cleaning up after Andrew's mess. It gave him a lot of time to think of a solution to this growing problem. Later that week he installed dead-bolt locks on all the fellowship hall doors to which he alone would have the keys.

When Friday night came and Andrew arrived at the church to set up for Fifth Quarter, he was met with Al's new addition to the facilities. Andrew didn't know why he was locked out. But he did know that there were forty pizzas and maybe two hundred students on their way. Thinking fast, he went into the storage room and grabbed several folding tables and dozens of folding chairs, which he set up in the parking lot. Sure enough, the students arrived *en masse* minutes later. Andrew patted himself on the back for his ingenuity in handling the situation. It started to rain as the party wound down, so he and the kids quickly carried the tables and chairs under the overhang of the church and left them there. Everyone had a great time, and Andrew felt as if he was really beginning to connect with a number of the students that had been coming every week. Most of the kids were showing up at the midweek Bible study, so Andrew felt he was really having a great spiritual impact on them.

When Al arrived Saturday afternoon, he wasn't worried about having to clean up the fellowship hall, but he was met with three brand-new folding tables that were ruined from sitting out in the rain. They hadn't quite made it under the overhang. Al exploded and called Jim, threatening to resign if the Fifth Quarter activities weren't cancelled.

Jim was surprised and disheartened by the situation. He was surprised by the intensity of Al's reaction. While he was thrilled with the ministry opportunities that Andrew had developed, he was disappointed that Andrew had not taken more responsibility in letting Al know what was happening and in cleaning up his messes.

Jim scheduled a meeting first thing Monday morning with Andrew and Al. Andrew had taken the Leading From Your Strengths® assessment, like you will have the opportunity to take in chapter 8, when he was being interviewed. Al had taken the assessment at a staff retreat several months before Andrew came on board. The senior pastor has both men's report on his desk, and an extra copy so they could take home and study the others report. At that meeting and in several others that week, the three were able to discuss what had happened. Andrew understood that his unscheduled events and his lack of responsibility for cleaning up were placing undue burdens on Al. Andrew apologized for his conduct and asked if Al would work with him to make sure that everything was done right in the future. Andrew also had the opportunity to explain to Al the ministry opportunities he had as a result of the Fifth Quarter parties. Al and his wife were active with high schoolers when their children were that age. The next week Al asked if he and his wife could attend the party. Andrew welcomed them.

That evening, when Al saw more than two hundred teens crammed into the fellowship hall, he thought of an idea to help relieve the crowding: putting more lights and a few basketball hoops in the parking lot. He got approval and had them installed before the next Friday night party. Al and his wife are now active partners with Andrew in the church's youth ministry.

STRENGTHS AND LIMITATIONS

Remember the core principles from chapter 2:

1. Understanding your own God-given strengths.
2. Recognizing and respecting the God-given strengths of those you work *with*.
3. Blending differences among team members.

As you look at the tables that follow, think of how you handle change and what your strengths and limitations may be, as well as those of your other team members. The charts also identify the sources of conflict that may occur on your team with team members who exhibit each of the different styles.

P R E D I C T A B L E	
STRENGTHS	
Good Team Player　　Stable Under Pressure　　Logical	
Patient　　Finishes Tasks　　Great Listener　　Methodical	
POTENTIAL LIMITATIONS	
Slow Paced　　Inflexible　　Controlling	
POTENTIAL SOURCES OF CONFLICT WITH OTHERS	
Lacks Sense of Urgency　　Avoids Confrontation	
Stubborn　　Actively Resists Change	
Apathetic　　Possessive of Information	

Team members with the predictable style are valuable to the team because of their natural desire to serve. Helping others actually energizes someone with the predictable style. They are patient and calm, with an inherent ability to hide their emotions.

Predictable people love to have stability and security in their lives. Those with the predictable style will not respond well to change unless they understand how and why the change is being made and have time to adjust. "We've always done it that way" is their motto. They would prefer the pace of activity on the team to be slower rather than faster.

Loyalty in relationships, whether business or personal, is a hallmark of the predictable style. Socially, predictable persons will have fewer relationships than the dynamic person, but typically the relationships are deeper and lifelong. Consistency and perseverance are also qualities of the predictable style. They prefer to do one project at a time, and they often avoid delegating because they want to finish what they start.

Predictable persons can sometimes be too slow paced. They desire to maintain a steady pace. Because of this, others may view them as obstacles to progress. Some may consider predictable persons as difficult to influence because of their nonemotional demeanor. Their demeanor can also make them seem close-minded to new ideas.

When pushed to an extreme, these potential limitations can lead to open conflict on a team. The predictable person can seem not only unemotional but also apathetic. Some may view them as lacking a sense of urgency. Team members can look at predictable team members as actively resisting change rather than simply questioning the true need for change.

D Y N A M I C	**STRENGTHS**			
	Energetic	Dynamic	Spontaneous	Flexible
	Involved	Versatile	Progressive	
	POTENTIAL LIMITATIONS			
	Impatient	Intense	Impulsive	
	Irresponsible	Restless	Hurried	
	POTENTIAL SOURCES OF CONFLICT WITH OTHERS			
	Unorganized	Everything Is a Priority	Insensitive	
	Lacks Follow-Through	Change for Change's Sake		

The dynamic person can bring incredible strengths to a team. These people can work at a fast pace, juggling many different projects at once. They are true multitaskers! They bring energy to the team along with their versatility. Dynamic people usually won't be overlooked or uninvolved. They are change agents who want to move forward rather than cling to the status quo. They prefer a fast-paced environment.

They can be emotional and expressive. The emotion of the dynamic person can escalate into an intensity that is unhealthy.

Their dynamic, energetic nature can become pressured, frenetic, hurried. This can lead to conflict with others who may view this as an inability to prioritize. It seems that everything is a high priority.

While the predictable person may be seen as resistant to change, the dynamic person is seen as someone who wants change just for the sake of change. This can lead to the dynamic person being labeled as unpredictable. In fact, it could lead to their being viewed as someone who can't be counted on.

Some team members may see the dynamic person as someone who starts projects but rarely finishes them. In the extreme, the dynamic person is impulsive and may jump from one project to another on a whim. This communicates to the more steady, predictable style that dynamic persons have little to no follow-up or follow-through.

Think about everyone on your team as you consider what you have learned from the tables. We encourage you to ask yourself these questions:

- How do you respond to change?
- How do your teammates respond to change?
- What are the strengths and limitations among you and your team members?
- How can you reduce conflict on your team by understanding the different strengths and limitations on your team?

Change can be difficult to handle for any team. Try going backward through major rapids sometime! What is important is knowing how the team will handle it. We need an understanding of our different strengths in dealing with change and a conscious effort to blend those strengths, striking a balance that ensures our team is running the river together.

Running the river with a spirit of unity becomes important as we head into day four.

Chapter Seven
The "Rules and Procedures" Transition

RIVER GUIDE'S DIARY: DAY FOUR

I PULLED THE TEAM TOGETHER *after breakfast to discuss what lay ahead on the river. We had a difficult decision to make right out of the chute this morning. The reason was the Great Divide, a large rock formation that splits the river in two for about half a mile. The south fork is the route that the National Park Service strongly recommends rafters take. In fact, the written rules of the rafting company require guides to take the south fork. The north fork is usually traveled only by professional kayakers and rafters who want an extreme rafting experience. There was nothing exceptionally difficult about any one of the rapids on the north fork, but having several difficult rapids in quick succession was what stopped most people from trying it. I was ready to try it today. I hadn't run the north fork for some time, but with the team I had now, I was sure we could do it.*

I briefly explained the situation and laid out the options for the team. I told them about the National Park Service recommendation and the rules of the rafting company. I assured them that the unwritten rule among the guides was to take the north fork if they felt their team could handle it. I told them that I believed this team could run the north fork, but it had to be their decision. They had to choose whether we played it safe and took the south fork or risked it and ran the north fork. I had a feeling which option most of my team would choose, but I made clear to them that if people ended up in the water on the north fork it could be dangerous.

Most of the team said they were ready to take on the rapids of the north fork. I told them that for us to take a shot at the north fork the decision had to be unanimous. To my surprise, only one of the team members expressed serious concerns. He was upset that we would go against the Park Service recommendation and openly violate the rules of the rafting company. He wasn't buying my explanation about the unwritten rule, and the fact that I had run the north fork several times without any problems didn't sway him. He peppered me with questions about the north fork and what we would be facing.

I could feel the tension in the raft as the discussion continued once we were in the river. Our holdout held his ground, but he knew he was on the hot seat. The National Park Service recommendation and the rules of the rafting company were his trump cards, and he kept playing them. It was easy to see that "rules are rules" was this guy's motto.

Our attention quickly returned to the river as we approached our first set of rapids for the day. It was helpful for me to get the team's focus back on the dangers and risks we were presently experiencing rather than on what lay ahead. Fortunately, the Colorado has an impressive ability to remind you of its presence.

After about a half hour, we could see the entrance to the Great Divide downriver. Then I remembered an overlook trail where we could scout out the Great Divide from above. We pulled ashore and set off up the overlook trail. It was a steep climb, and the temperature made me wish we were back in the water, but we could finally get a good look at both sides of the Divide. From our vantage point I pointed out all the trouble spots on the north fork and told them how I would guide us through.

Our holdout kept asking questions, but now I was able to give him more detailed information about our prospects. I walked them through the river again. I pointed out all the *obstacles, told them how I would lead them through, what they were going to need to do, and when they would need to do it. There was silence, and all eyes fell on our holdout. He nodded his head and then mumbled "OK, let's go." His response was not overwhelmingly confident, but the collective chorus of cheers that followed was. We all got back to the raft quickly before he could change his mind.*

As we came into the entrance of the north fork, I could tell the river was running high speed. I barked out orders, which helped us avoid some big rocks. Next we hit a hole just as ugly as the one yesterday. Without having to be told, two of my river-eaters went to the front of the raft as we dug in for a wild ride. The next ten minutes seemed like ten seconds as we were swept from rapid to rapid. I could tell that our scouting session had paid dividends.

Once we passed the end of the Great Divide, the team was ecstatic. It had been a wild ride, but we worked together and did it. About an hour later, we pulled in to set up camp. We were still sky high with excitement from our accomplishment. That night for dinner I had another surprise for them—steak! As we ate, some of the hard-core rafters admitted that scouting the rapids beforehand had been a great idea and really helped them on the river.

Tomorrow is our last day on the river, and our trip ends, as always, with Crystal Rapids—our biggest challenge yet.

The last unavoidable rapid is the Risk Transition. Every team has rules, procedures, and constraints that its members must deal with. How they deal with them is the key to the risk transition.

Some team members, like our holdout rafter, are going to operate by the book. They naturally follow established rules and procedures in their business and personal lives. They are usually critical thinkers who test the ideas of others and often ask for more information before agreeing to them. They set high standards for themselves and have a strong desire for the team to live up to the same standards.

Other team members will consistently challenge the status quo. They are much more independent and willing to bend or break the rules, which they may see as standing in the way of the team reaching its goals. They are not concerned with the consequences of doing so. They tend to make quick decisions, not waiting to gather all the facts before they do. They are naturally willing to take risks.

The predictable conflicts that arise as a result of these differing styles can affect every ministry team. Too much emphasis on following rules and procedures or analyzing every last detail can paralyze a team. *Keep in mind, we're not talking about debating biblical commands and admonitions.* God's Word is inviolate, and his truth isn't up for debate. Sin is always sin. Yet aside from God's Word and rules for life, there are hundreds of "rule books" that have to be written and rewritten to fit different situations in life and ministry.

Like the rule book for running the river in the story that started this chapter, there are often written or unwritten rules that are a part of each church and ministry culture. For example, in some churches or ministries, just tossing a receipt on the business administrator's desk is enough to get a reimbursement. Try that at another church without filling out the right forms, and your credit card bill would never be paid!

In some ministry cultures, going outside the box is a great way to gain a promotion. In other settings there's a word for people who forget the rules or don't follow them—it's *unemployed!*

Think about your team. Knowing the different strengths of each team member in regards to their bent to follow "standard procedures" or go around them is yet another key to understanding predictable conflict within a team. It can also help a team prevent team paralysis or conflict in the first place and enable each of the team members to lead from their strengths.

GO BY THE PLAYBOOK,
OR DRAW A NEW PLAY ON THE GROUND

A classic example of the push/pull in many groups when it comes to following a rule book happened to a large, established church. The longtime senior pastor unexpectedly passed away. After a time of shock and mourning, a search committee was formed to find a successor.

The first thing this committee wrestled with was whether it was best for the church to look for someone with the same personality and skill set as the recently deceased senior pastor or someone very different. If the skill set needed was that of the previous pastor, the search would be a short one. Already on staff were two longtime assistant pastors who were much like their friend and mentor.

From the beginning, the committee was split on this issue. Some committee members wanted someone new, a breath of fresh air, while others wanted to stay with what they knew and liked. Some wanted someone who would bring in drama and move away from traditional worship music; others felt such a change would be too radical. However, before the debate went too far, something dramatic happened.

From out of the blue, the church received a call from one of that denomination's best-known pastors. This was a man who had built a large ministry from humble beginnings and had written books that had been used in hundreds of ministries.

No doubt about it, their church was growing and in a growth area in their city that spoke of a bright future. But as a midsize church, to have the opportunity to get a leader of that caliber seemed to be a golden opportunity.

The chairman of the search committee called this well-known leader, and they spent almost two hours on the phone. He wasn't just expressing an interest in coming; he said he had prayed about it and was ready to come in lieu of a call. The search committee members were beside themselves with excitement until they heard the one demand this pastor placed on his coming.

The well-known pastor needed a decision within the week. Forget the countless interviews, preaching in the pulpit, second visits, and committee dinners. This man felt that his years of visible service, not to mention his writing and speaking, said it all. They had a week to decide if he was God's man for their church. Despite the time pressure, the news energized the search committee, and instantly the committee was almost unanimous in favor of selecting this denominational superstar—almost.

Two members, who were in favor of hiring one of the assistant pastors, raised vigorous objections to the hurried selection process. They objected that the search couldn't be deliberate, no due diligence had been done on this candidate, no one on the committee had talked with his staff or deacons. Even if they did have a chance to nab a star preacher, they felt the decision was being made much too quickly, with virtually no basis other than the candidate's popularity.

Their pleas fell on deaf ears. Tempers flared as the two sides became entrenched in their positions. The chairman of the search committee argued strongly that this candidate would be able to take the church to a new level, expanding the church's present reach. The two dissenters stuck to their guns, arguing that the conservative, low-key style of their longtime pastor should be maintained.

Things deteriorated quickly. As word leaked out of the committee about the possibility of calling this noted pastor, excited calls to the church and search committee members urged them to act. The chairman decided that the time had come to take drastic action. He called a meeting of the committee and informed everyone that he was doing away with the precedent of having unanimous decisions on pastoral candidates. He was calling for a vote. The two dissenters protested, but the chairman was insistent that the unanimous decision rule had been a gentlemen's agreement and, therefore, could be changed by him informally. (In fact, unanimity wasn't a written rule in their church bylaws). So he called for a vote, and the well-known pastor was called in less than one month and actually preached his first sermon at his new church within two months.

The church was packed to overflowing on this man's first Sunday. Nine months later people were leaving the church in droves. That's because this superstar pastor had resigned in disgrace after being involved in a moral failure with a member of the congregation. It wasn't even a surprise later when the search committee found out that this behavior was something he'd done at his previous church, and fear of discovery had lead to his unexpected telephone call.

Following rules and standard procedures can provide a tremendous layer of protection for people and ministries. In this case it could have avoided a church split.

STRENGTHS AND LIMITATIONS

The way team members approach rules and procedures can have a profound impact on the team. Team members that learn this about themselves and others on the team are going to be more effective. This is why the core principles we introduced in chapter 2 are so important to remember:

1. Understanding your own God-given strengths.
2. Recognizing and respecting the God-given strengths of those you work *with.*
3. Blending differences among team members.

As you review the following tables, consider the strengths and limitations of each style as it relates to how people approach rules and procedures. Some people desire to follow rules and procedures, and some are willing to break them. When these two styles collide, conflict is inevitable. "Potential Sources of Conflict with Others" lists some of the ways that this conflict will manifest itself.

C O N S E R V A T I V E			
	STRENGTHS		
	Conscientious	High Standards	Fact-finder
	Analytical	Conservative	Cautious
	POTENTIAL LIMITATIONS		
	Slow Decision Making	Exacting	Perfectionist
	Overanalyzes	Oppressive	
	POTENTIAL SOURCES OF CONFLICT WITH OTHERS		
	Indecisive	Close-Minded	Unyielding
	Causes Gridlock	Critical	Distrusting

People with a conservative style tend to follow established rules and procedures in all areas of their lives. They are conscientious people with high standards for themselves and others. Those with a conservative style believe there is a right way and a wrong way of doing things, and they are constantly trying to find the right way. In addition, they are precise and exacting, with great attention to detail. If you want to influence the conservative person, make sure you have proof to back up what you say. They are not swayed by emotion or lots of words; rather, they want facts and figures to verify what they are told. They prefer this information to be in writing and from a reliable source. When questioning others, they are good at asking the right questions and getting to the heart of an issue.

The conservative person's dedication to doing things right can become a limitation in certain circumstances. Sometimes when asked to do a specific task, they will become hesitant to act unless they feel they have all the facts. This may also occur because they are simply overanalyzing the situation.

When interacting with others on the team, a conservative person can cause conflict by being too analytical. They hold themselves to a high standard of always doing things the right way, and they project these same standards onto others. People with other styles of behavior may not be as precise, and if the conservative person reacts to that, interpersonal conflict is likely. On the other hand, the conservative person can be defensive when criticized. This can be a disappointing source of conflict on a team as well.

At times conservative team members can be seen as unyielding or obstinate. Others may view them as so set in their ways that they are unable to take advantage of opportunities right before them. This can be extremely frustrating for others on the team who want to move forward more quickly.

	STRENGTHS		
I	Self-Reliant	Decisive	Questions Status Quo
N	Independent	Bold	Risk-Taker
D			
E	**POTENTIAL LIMITATIONS**		
P	Ignores Consequences	Impatient	Out of Control
E	Insensitive	Controversial	Unorganized
N			
D	**POTENTIAL SOURCES OF CONFLICT WITH OTHERS**		
E	Reckless	Overconfident	Indifferent
N	Overlooks Details	Haphazard	
T			

The strengths of the independent person, not surprisingly, revolve around the ability to think independently. Independent people are the "out of the box" thinkers and may even be seen as pioneering. They are not bound by maintaining the status quo, and, therefore, the independent person believes there is always a better ways of doing things, and that is the way they want to do them.

The independent style is bold and willing to take risks. To achieve their goals, they may be willing to break established rules and procedures (not laws and especially not God's laws, but rules and procedures put in place by others).

This independent style can lead others to view them as insensitive to the feelings of others, controversial, or even out of control. This can lead to conflict when others on the team tire of the independent person's pushing the envelope and bending or breaking the rules. The independent person can exacerbate the situation while seeming to ignore the consequences of their actions.

The other area of likely conflict with the independent style is when team members view them as reckless or haphazard. Independent thinkers are confident they will find a way to reach the team's goals, but they are often indifferent to the means to achieve the desired ends. This overconfidence can engender conflict on the team, especially when the independent thinker turns out to be wrong. Others on the team simply want the rules to apply to everyone, including the independent person.

As you examine the tables, consider how you and your team handle established rules and procedures. We encourage you to answer these questions about yourself and your team:

- How do you approach established rules and procedures?
- How do others on your team react to established rules and procedures?
- What are the strengths and limitations on your team as it relates to rules and procedures?
- What can you and your team do to capitalize on these different strengths to make the team more effective?

Chapter Eight

Life Lessons from the River

RIVER GUIDE'S DIARY: DAY FIVE

I LOVE THE EARLY MORNING HOURS *the best. Even the sounds of the river are quieter at sunrise. The warm rays of sun are a stark contrast to the brisk morning breeze that comes with it. This morning I soaked it in. I closed my eyes and thought back over my years of guiding on the Colorado. I remember my first day like it was yesterday. I will always come back to the river, but not as a guide anymore. The thought of not retiring tempts me, but I know twenty-five years is enough. My son will become a lead guide next year, and I know it's time to go.*

But not just yet. There was still one more exciting, glorious day to guide a team on the river. This last day was filled with difficult rapids: Salt Creek, Pipe Creek, Granite Rapids, and Crystal Rapids—one of the few rapids in the Grand Canyon rated a full ten—just waiting for us to come and test our skill and strength. Time to wake my team!

It was an hour before we hit the first set of rapids at Pipe Creek. At this point in the canyon, a number of streams flow into the river, making the water wildly unpredictable. While you can see some of the action on top of the water, it's what's underneath that concerned me most.

As we neared the first set of rapids, I shouted for everyone to dig in hard as I steered for the left side of the river. The undercurrent was pushing us left toward a huge rock, but our strong paddling saved us again. We were turned a little sideways when we hit some bigger waves. We almost lost one rafter in front on the left side. She managed to keep her foot wedged under the gear we had strapped down which gave her time to regain her balance.

Granite Rapids came hard on the heels of Pipe Creek. With everyone digging in, we hit a wave that stood the raft almost completely upright. Everyone, including me, held on for dear life, but amazingly, nobody was tossed out. The raft landed on its right side and came down hard on the left. We all ended up on the floor of the raft, and we had to move fast to get back in position as we rode out the rest of the waves. As we finished the roughest rapids, I felt grateful we had all stayed in the raft. Everyone breathed a collective sigh of relief.

A mile downstream, we were able to land at a small beach to rest and take in a quick lunch. Everyone devoured their lunch and was eager to get back on the river. This surprised me given the experiences of the morning. Before putting back in, I went over the next rapids and set up the raft to make sure the team was properly positioned. I put two of our strongest paddlers up front and two more in the back with me. This way, we had strong positions to move us through the river as the situation demanded.

It was another half hour before we came to Crystal Rapids. The most intimidating feature is called The Big Valley, where the water cuts deep in the middle and the waves stand up on both sides at least ten feet high. The entrance to The Big Valley is fast; there is no time to adjust. You either hit it right, or things get ugly fast.

We were lined up perfectly for The Big Valley. We hit the entrance dead center and shot right through. There were some wide eyes as we sailed past the two massive walls of water on each side. No matter how good the team was, no raft was going to make it if they hit one of those waves. I told everyone to stop paddling, and we rode out the rest of the rapids. Everyone was shouting and giving high fives when we finished Crystal Rapids.

We put into base camp late in the afternoon, where the support staff greeted us. Our trip was done and so was I. We packed our gear into the waiting helicopter, and flew out with a big cloud of dust. We could see the rapids we had just run as we gained altitude. They looked harmless from the air, but having seen them firsthand at water level, we knew different. I could tell everyone was thinking the same thing from the big grins on their faces. Once we were back at Lee's Ferry, we said our good-byes and posed for a group picture. I grabbed my things and headed for the River School building to check out for the last time. At the door I turned to look back at the river. I took a long look before opening the door and stepping into darkness.

It wasn't supposed to be dark. I fumbled for the light switch, but someone beat me to it. As the lights came on and a cheer went up, I stood there staring wide-eyed at every guide I had worked with over the last twenty-five years. My wife and son were holding a huge cake shaped like a white-water raft with "John Carter, River Guide" and a big "25" in the middle. My eyes were still blurry, but not from the lights . . .

John Carter's last team of white-water rafters made it through their trip on the Colorado with a lifetime of memories. John's last trip with an inexperienced team was one of his best, and he added some great memories to his considerable collection.

John never tired of the river because it was different every day. There were always new obstacles to avoid, unexpected decisions to be made, and usually enough close calls to make things interesting. John's description of the river may sound a lot like a description of the way your ministry team operates.

John would have said the same thing about every team he led. Each team had a different personality. Each team member had natural strengths and limitations. John used his knowledge about those strengths and limitations to successfully navigate his raft through the rapids. He often changed his strategies by knowing each rafter's particular strengths and limitations and using them to meet unforeseen conditions on the river. You can do this with your ministry team by using the same principles.

THE LEADING FROM YOUR STRENGTHS® PROCESS

There is a reason your ministry team operates the way it does, and it relates to the strengths and limitations of each team member. For many teams the strengths and limitations of each team member are never examined. The result can be a constant state of problems, conflict, or simply ineffectiveness. Without such an examination the source of these issues remains a mystery, and finding a solution that works is difficult if not impossible.

The Leading From Your Strengths® process uncovers the source of a great many team problems, conflicts, and ineffectiveness through an examination of the strengths and limitations of each team member. The process begins with self-examination and progresses to include team-building exercises where everyone shares his or her God-given strengths with others on their team. Team members can also share their limitations with one another. Team members can protect the limitations of others by using their strengths to offset another's weakness. Only then is the team capable of fully capitalizing on the strengths of the whole team to achieve maximum effectiveness. Only then is the team really able to understand sources of conflict and how to resolve them.

Conflict on your team is predictable based on the respective styles of the individuals that make up your team (not to mention our sin nature!). Knowing the default setting of each person on your team can enable you to identify predictable conflict and reduce or eliminate it. The same is true for miscommunication that occurs because of style differences. Understanding the style of others on your team allows effective communication to become the norm.

The Leading From Your Strengths® process starts with you. The most effective people are those who understand how God has created them and just who they are in living out their own unique gifts and strengths. The Leading From Your Strengths® assessment will help you gain this knowledge about yourself and apply it in building bridges with others on your team.

Where do we begin in gaining the kind of crucial knowledge we'll need not only to stay afloat but to succeed as a team? By defining some terms that we use in the powerful online assessment that's a crucial part of the Leading From Your Strengths® process.

Dr. John Trent has taught the principles behind the Leading From Your Strengths® assessment for more than twenty years. He developed a unique way of describing the behavioral styles we have discussed in a fun, informative, and memorable way. He first used the animal characters of Lion, Otter, Golden Retriever, and Beaver in his book _The Two Sides of Love,_ and has since used them in seminars across the country to teach people about their God-given strengths.

Today Dr. Trent has teamed with Rodney Cox, the Leading From Your Strengths® teaching team, to use these same four word pictures combined with sophisticated, state-of-the art online assessments. The result is an unparalleled way of helping people understand their unique, God-given strengths and style, as well as the styles of others. While we'll go into more detail later, here's how these word pictures correlate to the obstacles that face teams every day:

- Lion (Problems and Challenges)
- Otter (People and Information)
- Golden Retriever (Pace and Change)
- Beaver (Rules and Procedures)

The Leading From Your Strengths® assessment will reveal your natural, God-given strengths in each of these areas. You will discover how you respond to problems, how you trust people and information, how you react to change, and how you approach rules and procedures. Your Leading From Your Strengths® report will be the primary building block for the whole Leading From Your Strengths® process. We believe that by investing just ten minutes to take your online report, the potential for your becoming a better team member, leader, and team is tremendous. In short, your investment of time will pay huge dividends of closeness and effectiveness as a God-honoring team!

TAKING THE ASSESSMENT

Now you are ready to discover your own unique strengths! To take the Leading From Your Strengths® assessment, go to www.leadingfromyourstrengths.com and click the "special offer" link. When prompted for your special code, type the word _strengths_ to recieve a discount on the purchase of the Leading From Your Strengths® assessment.

The Leading From Your Strengths® assessment should be taken in one sitting and should take ten minutes or less to complete. While taking the online assessment, focus on your role in your ministry team. After you finish taking this instrument, your Leading From Your Strengths® report will be generated within seconds and will be almost instantly viewable on-screen and available for printing! No sending in papers or waiting for a Ph.D. to go over what your report means. The report comes to you in understandable English and will also be e-mailed to the e-mail address you specify when you take the assessment. Taking the Leading From Your Strengths® assessment is that easy!

We encourage you to take your Leading From Your Strengths® assessment right now before moving on to chapter 9!

Chapter Nine
Into the River and On with Your Journey!

★

NOW THAT YOU'VE COMPLETED your Leading From Your Strengths®
assessment, you're ready to get into the raft and confront the unique
challenges facing *your* ministry team. The next four chapters are
designed to help you draw out the most from your online assessment by identifying your God-given strengths and limitations, helping you identify those traits in others, and giving you practical
suggestions on how to use these insights to overcome obstacles that
arise from predictable areas of conflict. You'll also be better equipped
to blend differences with others on your team and build stronger
relationships and a more effective ministry team as a result.

As you progress through the next several chapters, keep in
mind that the body of Christ does not have one part, but many.
The strengths you discover about yourself are important to your
team, but not more important than others on the team. We are
created to use our God-given strengths to serve God and others,
not ourselves. (See 1 Corinthians 12:12–26.) Use your strengths
to complete the limitations of others, that they may be built up.
(See Romans 15:1–12.)

So, with all this in mind, let's "dive in"!

We want to guide you step-by-step through each major section of your twenty-eight-page report. As we move through each
section of your report, we will be asking you to reflect on how
the personalized information impacts you and your team.

Here's our promise to you that comes right from the Book of Proverbs: "Acquire wisdom—how much better it is than gold!" The writer says, "And acquire understanding—it is preferable to silver" (16:16). While your online assessment is a great value added to this book, we've seen time and again that the insights gained from taking it and completing the process become priceless to an individual, team, or church.

UNDERSTANDING YOUR LEADING FROM YOUR STRENGTHS® ONLINE ASSESSMENT

If you turn to page 4 of your personal report, you will see your Core Style Graph. This graph is a snapshot of the data gathered from your responses. To be able to communicate effectively to everyone taking a Leading From Your Strengths® assessment, we have incorporated three important graphic elements to better help you understand what your report is saying.

The first element is the range of numbers running up the left side of the graph in figure 1. What these numbers represent is the percentage of your score in each of the four columns. The next element is the Energy Line that runs horizontally through the graph. In our strengths assessment model, we look at plot points both above *and* below the line. The farther away your plot points are from the Energy Line, either above it or below it, the more strongly you will tend to exhibit the corresponding character traits on a daily basis, and the more difficult it will be to adapt your behavior to a position on the other side of the Energy Line. The final element is the four vertical lines

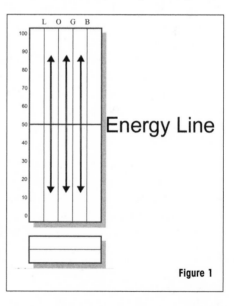

Figure 1

designated by the letters *L, O, G,* and *B.* Each of these lines is tied to one of the four transitions facing ministry teams discussed previously:

L represents the Lion characteristic—problems and challenges.

O represents the Otter characteristic—people and information.

G represents the Golden Retriever characteristic—pace and change.

B represents the Beaver characteristic—rules and procedures.

Your Leading From Your Strengths® assessment indicates your score and charts the corresponding percentages in each of these four columns on page 4.

With these three elements in mind, let's briefly look at the results from a hypothetical assessment from a pastor we'll call Robert. Looking at the graph in figure 2, you will see that Robert scored a 70 percent on the Lion scale, 90 percent on the Otter scale, 25 percent on the Golden Retriever scale, and 40 percent on the Beaver scale.

Each of the points both above and below the scale tells us about the predictable way Robert will act. These actions are observable and can be better understood and described by looking at the descriptors listed in figure 3.

Look at the descriptors that fall around the 70 percentile range on the Lion scale (outlined with the circle on the column). You will see that Robert's score correlates with the following traits: Driving, Ambitious, Forceful, and Determined. Moving to the next column of the graph, the Otter scale, we see that Robert scores high at 90 percent. Looking at the descriptor column in figure 3,

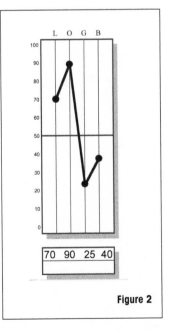

ROBERT

Figure 2

Lion	Otter	Golden Retriever	Beaver
Demanding	Effusive	Phlegmatic	Evasive
Egocentric	Inspiring	Relaxed	Worrisome
		Resistant to Change	Careful
Driving	Magnetic	Nondemonstrative	Dependent
Ambitious	Political		Cautious
Pioneering	Enthusiastic	Passive	Conventional
Strong-Willed	Demonstrative		Exacting
Forceful	Persuasive	Patient	Neat
Determined	Warm		
Aggressive	Convincing	Possessive	Systematic
Competitive	Polished		Diplomatic
Decisive	Poised	Predictable	Accurate
Venturesome	Optimistic	Consistent	Tactful
		Deliberate	
Inquisitive	Trusting	Steady	Open-Minded
Responsible	Sociable	Stable	Balanced Judgment
Conservative	Reflective	Mobile	Firm
Calculating	Factual	Active	Independent
Cooperative	Calculating	Restless	Self-Willed
Hesitant	Skeptical	Alert	Stubborn
Low-Keyed		Variety-Oriented	
Unsure	Logical	Demonstrative	Obstinate
Undemanding	Undemonstrative		
Cautious	Suspicious	Impatient	Opinionated
	Matter-of-Fact	Pressure-Oriented	Unsystematic
Mild	Incisive	Eager	Self-Righteous
Agreeable		Flexible	Uninhibited
Modest	Pessimistic	Impulsive	Arbitrary
Peaceful	Moody	Impetuous	Unbending
Unobtrusive	Critical	Hypertense	Careless with Details

Figure 3

we see that the characteristics associated with this level on the scale (highlighted with the circle) are Demonstrative, Enthusiastic, Magnetic, and Persuasive.

At this point we can see Robert's natural tendencies emerge from the scores in each area. For example, now that we know Robert's Otter tendency is higher than his Lion tendency, we could say that Robert is first Inspiring, Enthusiastic, and Persuasive, and second Ambitious, Forceful, and Determined. Therefore Robert will persuade people to his point of view aggressively looking to the agreement of others and the bottom line to measure the results.

The next column in figure 3 is the Golden Retriever. This scale speaks to how people deal with pace and change. Here Robert's score is 25 percent. Robert is going to be Alert, Impatient, Eager, and Flexible. We can see why Robert will actively seek others to communicate with and will build relationships with a variety of people. These relationships will typically be more superficial and will be used by Robert as a platform to discuss the changes he sees as important to his success. Anxious and impatient to overcome obstacles, Robert will want be involved in all decisions, and his opinions may be expressed in an emotional manner.

Finally, the Beaver scale, the last column in figure 3, shows that Robert has scored 40 percent. When it comes to rules and procedures, Robert is going to be Firm, Independent, Stubborn, and Self-Willed. With this low Beaver tendency, we can say that Robert is confident and relaxed with others, even in social situations that may seem risky or uncertain. Robert sees people for what they can do for him rather than as a hindrance. He will tend to involve other people to accomplish his goals. Robert will aggressively and independently tackle problems with little regard for possible drawbacks in choice of solutions. He will do so without checking to see how it has been done in the past.

Now let's look at what it would mean if Robert had scored lower in one of the scales in figure 3. Let's say his score was 35 percent on the Lion scale, meaning that he would tend to exhibit the following traits: Undemanding, Low-Keyed, and Cautious.

What is different about these descriptors compared to the descriptors we discussed in this column originally? They are not only different; they are opposite! In understanding the LOGB model of behavior, as well as understanding your own graph, it is important to understand that the position of the plot points on each scale is important to how we analyze people's natural tendencies and appreciate who they are.

Take a look now at your Core Style Graph on page 4 of your Leading From Your Strengths® report. Look at the plot point in each of the LOGB columns and find the descriptors in figure 3 that correspond to those plot points. We encourage you to write them down. The descriptors will give you a quick snapshot of who God made you to be and your natural behavioral tendencies.

Let's go deeper into how these tendencies specifically blend together and how fearfully and wonderfully God made you. (See Psalms 139:13–14a.) You are not just a Lion, Otter, Golden Retriever, or Beaver; you are a unique combination of each style!

GENERAL CHARACTERISTICS SECTION OF YOUR ONLINE REPORT

The rest of this chapter will focus on a few of the major sections of your report. After each section is reviewed, there will be a set of questions. We encourage you to answer these questions for yourself and to record your answers. As we stated earlier, an easy way to do that is to download the Leading From Your Strengths® Teambuilding Workbook by clicking on the Free Downloads button in the left-hand menu bar of the www.leading fromyourstrengths.com Web site. If you prefer, you can simply record your answers on a separate sheet of paper. Whatever method you use, we encourage you to record your answers so you can share them with your team at the appropriate time.

Let's examine the information contained in your report. What your Core Style Graph gives is a broad indication of the natural way you go about doing things. The Core Style Graph is interpreted in the General Characteristics section in detailed written form. The General Characteristics section will also highlight how you tend to respond under stress in a ministry team context. It's also important to note that this analysis is highly specific to your unique God-given personality. The assessment you've taken online has the ability to produce 19,860 separate combinations of Core Style Graphs distilled into 384 distinct behavioral styles, each with its own unique differences. That means your report will be specific to you and accurate in reflecting your true nature.

Turn to pages 5–6 and review your General Characteristics thoroughly. Once you have done this, answer these questions to draw out those specific elements of your report that you think best reflect your strengths.

Your selections are designed to help you recognize your core strengths, the predictable ways you would choose to carry out your

---

From the General Characteristics section of your report, which three statements from each paragraph (nine total) cause you to nod your head and say to yourself, "That's me!"?

In your own words, what do you believe is the number one strength you bring to the team?

How do you see this strength being lived out on your team?

In this section, have you identified any areas where you need personal and spiritual growth?

work and relate to others. This may be the first time you have had the opportunity to pinpoint accurately what your strengths really are. In the following pages and chapters, we'll highlight many more specific elements that can help you document your natural approach in handling a wide variety of situations and conflicts.

"VALUE TO THE TEAM" SECTION OF YOUR ONLINE REPORT

Now turn to page 7 of your Leading From Your Strengths® report. This section reveals the practical assets that you bring to your ministry team. By looking at these statements, you can better understand the specific talents you bring to the ministry, as well as how you can better use those talents. This is also an important section to share with others on your team to help highlight, for each person, his or her unique contributions to your team.

Capitalizing on this information, you can help your team operate more efficiently and effectively. All of these elements are important because one of the most difficult things for individuals to do is to communicate their talents to others. Particularly in Christian settings, keeping God's Word in mind—"Let another praise you and not your own mouth" (see Proverbs 27:2)—your Leading From Your Strengths® report can become a powerful way for you and others on your team to see valuable traits you have and can bring to your team. As you read through this section of your report, answer the following questions:

1. Which four statements best describe the value you bring to the team?

2. On a scale of 1 to 10, (1 meaning very little, 10 meaning a great deal), how do you feel your talents are currently being used on your team?

3. Are there any strengths that you are not using as much as you should?

4. What do you need to do to make others aware of these strengths?

5. How would using those strengths make a positive difference to your team?

"IDEAL ENVIRONMENT" SECTION
OF YOUR ONLINE REPORT

This next section is intended to help you see the type of work atmosphere that best suits your style and strengths. In order to perform at our best, we need a nurturing, natural environment to maximize our performance. For example, if you maintained a fish tank at home, you wouldn't purchase expensive saltwater fish and put them in a freshwater tank. Nor would you buy large saltwater fish and put them in a little fishbowl filled with tap water. This would be a severe restraint on the natural growth of the fish—not to mention cutting down on their odds of survival!

As people, we operate in much the same way when it comes to the "ideal environment" we live or work in. That's not to say that we can't adapt as people or that we can't function if our ministry environment isn't a perfect match for us. But this section will give you, and others, a look at what would be ideal for you to grow and contribute and provides some clear goals and insights that are important to you and your team. Page 12 in your report highlights your ideal environment—that is, the environment you need to be in to perform at an optimal level and flourish. Using these statements from your online report, answer the following questions:

---

1. Which three statements from your report seem best to describe your ideal environment?

2. Which, if any, of these conditions are not being met in your current environment?

3. What actions could you take that will lead to meeting or communicating some of these conditions in your current environment? Please be as specific as possible.

"KEYS TO MOTIVATING" SECTION OF
YOUR ONLINE REPORT

People tend to be motivated by the things they want, need, or highly value. Even as committed believers, if we're in a situation where we feel that our efforts don't count, or we aren't appreciated, or our thoughts or actions aren't valued, it can lead to halfhearted efforts over time, and often we'll see the level of our performance drop. On page 13 of your online report, you'll see several statements that will help you understand what specific things motivate you, as well as highlight some of the frustrations you may be feeling. Some of this information would be appropriate to share with other team members, while other information should only be shared with your team leader. If you are the team leader, this is valuable information for you to see and understand about those you're shepherding.

As you move through the following questions, think carefully about how this information from your report could be helpful to you and your team.

---

1. What are the top three statements from your "keys to motivating" that seem to strike a chord with you?

2. Do the statements you chose have anything in common? If so, what?

3. To whom will you specifically communicate these desires and values so that they might understand more clearly how to create an environment that motivates you?

"Keys to Leading" Section
of Your Online Report

Most of us have experienced the discouragement and disappointing feelings that come from being led by someone who doesn't understand us or seem to value what we need. In most cases, leaders don't mismanage people on purpose. Whether it's being busy or simply not knowing how to understand the things that motivate others, reporting relationships becomes a matter of trial and error. That's a great way to cause frustration in a ministry or workplace setting. The critical element to this section of your online report is how it can help us communicate to those in leadership above us the keys to using our strengths most effectively. In communicating our strengths and weaknesses to our leaders and others around us, we can break down the barriers that might be leading to undue conflict and stress in our lives. Work through these questions that can hold significant insights for an effective team:

1. Which statements in this section do you feel must be met in order for you to perform at an optimal level?

2. Do you feel that any of these needs are not currently being met?

3. To whom specifically should you communicate this, and when will you do it?

You've now worked through a number of key areas of your report that can give you and the other people on your team important insights into your strengths, communication style, and much more. As important as this information is, there is more to come. So let's look at another important part of your Leading From Your Strengths® report, which can hold additional powerful personal insights.

Chapter Ten
Core and Adapted Styles

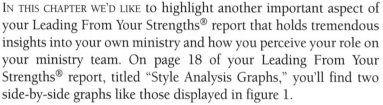

IN THIS CHAPTER WE'D LIKE to highlight another important aspect of your Leading From Your Strengths® report that holds tremendous insights into your own ministry and how you perceive your role on your ministry team. On page 18 of your Leading From Your Strengths® report, titled "Style Analysis Graphs," you'll find two side-by-side graphs like those displayed in figure 1.

We've already highlighted your Core Style Graph and how it displays the real you when it comes to your natural tendencies of behavior. Your Core Graph will tend to stay the same over time. This does not mean that it can't change somewhat in intensity in each of the animal styles, but a dramatic change normally won't happen unless you experience a life-changing personal event such as the death of a spouse or child. In figure 1, Steve's Core Graph has three plot

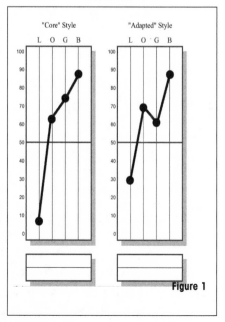

STEVE

Figure 1

points above the Energy Line. He's high on the Otter, even higher on the Golden Retriever, and highest on the Beaver. His natural behavior or Core Style will be relational (high Otter), highly sensitive to others (high Golden Retriever), with high standards and expectations for himself and others (high Beaver). With his Lion score very low, Steve doesn't use force of character to influence others. He can let someone else set the goal or vision and then can do a great job of verbally encouraging, being sensitive to the needs of others, and maintaining high standards and expectations. But look now at his Adapted Style Graph.

What Do I Feel I Need to Do to Be Successful in My Ministry?

The Adapted Style Graph allows you to look at any differences there may be between who Steve is in his core strengths and how he feels he needs to adapt to be successful in meeting the demands placed on him in ministry. Look again at Steve's side-by-side graphs and note the differences.

For Steve there is little adaptation between his core strengths and what he feels his ministry situation demands of him to be successful. In real life, Steve is an assistant education pastor. As you can see, the person he is when he wakes up in the morning (core strengths) is nearly identical to the person he feels he needs to be to adapt to the demands of his job.

The Adapted Style Graph for Steve shows that his Lion goes up slightly but is still low. In his ministry setting Steve reports to the head education pastor, who sets the direction and goals. On the Otter scale on his Adapted Style Graph, again Steve's scores are almost the same. Because Steve at times has to say no to volunteers and others, his Golden Retriever sensitivity goes down slightly on his Adapted Style Graph. And his Beaver score goes up slightly, meaning his natural tendency to do things right and in a quality way is what he feels is demanded of him in order to succeed in this ministry setting.

When Your Core and Adapted Style Is Similar

For Steve, and perhaps for you if your Core and Adapted Graphs are similar, there is likely a close match between who you are in your core strengths and who you feel you have to become to succeed in ministry. In most cases that's an indication that what you're doing is close to a natural fit for who you are. The behavioral demands and expectations of the role you are playing in the ministry matches your God-shaped behavioral design.

Does this mean that every day Steve shows up to work is a walk in the park? Absolutely not! With his Beaver so high, both core and adapted, Steve has high expectations of himself and others, and he has a Lion boss who can change directions on him at times. Yet in most cases, people like Steve whose Core and Adapted Graphs are similar will have to expend less emotional energy to live out what they think it takes to succeed in their ministry.

WHEN YOUR CORE AND ADAPTED SCORES ARE DIFFERENT

Let's look at another assistant education pastor, whose Core and Adapted Graphs shift significantly and aren't a mirror image of each other. In fact, for most people, you'll see a moderate shift show up on these two graphs.

As we look at Rick's Core Graph in figure 2, he's low on the Otter scale, meaning he's hesitant to verbalize his thoughts and feelings. What stands out in Rick's case is a Golden

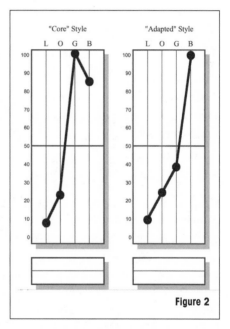

RICK

Figure 2

Retriever score that's right at the top, in the Mother Theresa range, when it comes to sensitivity and caring! Rick is, at his core, tremendously sensitive to others and their needs and feelings, and he also has fairly high expectations of himself and others, as you can see in his high Beaver score.

Now look at Rick's Adapted Graph. In the church where Rick works, there's a huge shift in his Adapted Style and what he feels is demanded of him to succeed. In his Core Style, Rick puts people over task (Golden Retriever over Beaver). Yet in the high-demand environment of Rick's ministry, things are really going fast and seem to be unpredictable. He would prefer to slow down and take one project at a time, but to keep pace in his environment, he can't. This internal conflict will make Rick uncomfortable and possibly stressed out. Rick's Golden Retriever score drops almost 70 points and crosses the Energy Line, and his Beaver score goes up even higher.

In your Leading From Your Strengths® report, any time you have a plot point cross the Energy Line, either up or down, that signals a significant shift. For Rick to succeed in a fast-paced ministry setting, he feels that he has to stay busy with a variety of projects. He feels he cannot focus on one project too long, but his work environment demands that he "dot all the i's and cross all the t's." He feels the need to put task over people. And, as is often the case when someone has to operate differently from their Core Style in order to be successful, that can raise the stress level and increase the energy expended on a daily basis. This leads to an important question.

Are Major Adaptations Good or Bad?

If you see a major shift between your Core and Adapted Graphs, these adaptations are important to see, talk through, pray over, and share with others on your team. In some cases this section of the Leading From Your Strengths® report alone has been the eye-opener that the Lord has used to point out areas of great stress or strain. It can indeed be difficult to operate outside our core or natural strengths in order to meet what we feel is expected of us to succeed in our ministry. *However, don't jump to the conclusion that every adaptation is negative!*

For example, look at another set of Core and Adapted Graphs that shows a major shift or adaptation.

Look at Barb's Core and Adapted Graphs in figure 3. You can see that when it comes to who she is when she wakes up and how she feels she has to adapt to succeed when she gets to her place of ministry, her Otter score drops almost 70 points, crossing the Energy Line. That's a significant shift. For example, if you were to go over to Barb's house for hamburgers on a weekend, you'd find her engaging and outgoing. But look at how she feels she needs to act to succeed in her ministry as a Christian counselor at her church.

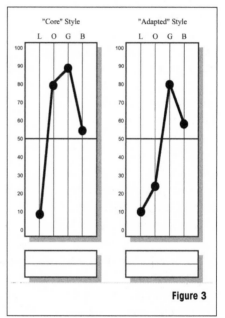

BARB

Figure 3

As a counselor, her job is to ask questions and dig deeper into understanding her clients behavior, rather than not taking what her clients tell her at face value. She can't indiscriminately trust the information she is receiving, and she needs to ask critical questions of her counselees. She needs to be more attentive, listening more than talking, which is not a bad thing for a counselor. In fact, for years, Barb has been a great listener and encourager and has discovered that asking hard questions can lead to great results. Again, while major adaptations certainly signal that we're having to expend more energy and, in many cases, that it's putting stress on us to act in ways where we may not have natural strengths, that's not always bad!

ADDITIONAL INSIGHTS FROM THESE SIDE-BY-SIDE GRAPHS

Not all major adaptations are caused by your current ministry environment. Major adaptations are often caused by influences in your personal life. Major adaptations can happen because of something as devastating as the loss of a loved one or something as subtle as a blow to your self-esteem. Larry is a prime example of someone who experienced this kind of major adaptation from his Core Style. Larry's Core and Adapted Graphs are in figure 4.

Larry is a ministry team leader who, when you look at his Core Graph, is right at the top when it comes to Lion characteristics. He's forceful, take-charge, assertive, and ready to take the lead; but that's balanced somewhat by a high score on the Golden Retriever scale. In short, Larry is a leader who may push or be too assertive at times, but he also cares about people. He realizes the need for relationship as well as getting things done.

Yet look at Larry's Core Graph one more time and

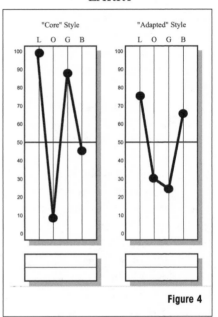

LARRY

Figure 4

see the dramatic V shape caused by the high Lion, low Otter, and high Golden Retriever plot points. In short, all that aggressiveness (super-high Lion) is mixed with a lack of trust and a hesitancy to share his thoughts or feelings (low Otter), as well as a sensitivity and alertness to the needs of others (high Golden Retriever).

Now look at Larry's Adapted Style Graph in figure 4. Larry's Lion stays strong; his Otter goes up somewhat; his Golden Retriever goes down, crossing the Energy Line; and his Beaver moves above the Energy Line. When Larry first saw his scores, he felt it described him perfectly. His Adapted Style was that of a high Lion/Beaver, meaning there's a right way (Beaver) and it's my way (Lion)! What happened to the sensitivity and concern for people of the high Golden Retriever?

The answer lies in a difficult experience from Larry's past. Larry was a company commander in the Gulf War before becoming a ministry leader. The trauma of war left him unable to open up and share the concerns, hurts, and sorrow that were part of his personal experience. This drained him of his ability to feel empathetic toward others.

As we took Larry through the Leading From Your Strengths® process, he saw that his Adapted Style—what he felt he had to do to succeed in ministry—was directly linked to his experiences, especially the kind of leader he served under in the war. Larry reported to an officer whose style was "Do it now, do it my way, and don't ask why." This was ingrained in him, and it was no wonder he struggled so much in his church!

Understanding how this past experience affected him finally got Larry talking about who God created him to be and how that was being lived out, or how he was adapting in his ministry. He started scheduling one-on-one time with his staff to talk through their issues and concerns. Needless to say, as Larry forced himself to share openly the information he learned during the Leading From Your Strengths® process, he not only began to see himself in a different light, but his team members saw him in a different light as well. He began asking for feedback from others and didn't look at his natural sensitivity as a weakness but used it to make him a better leader and encourager as he ministered to the people God had placed in his life.

"How Are You Having to Adapt?" Section
of Your Online Report

It's time to look closer now at how you are adapting your style to succeed in ministry. The next part of your Leading From Your Strengths® report is one of the most instructive and helpful sections. It can highlight clues to where and why you might experience stress in your ministry, related to how much you are having to adapt in your current ministry environment. While your core graph is typically fixed unless there is a life-changing event, each new ministry situation or change in your ministry role might require you to make adaptations in each of the four animal styles. _Adapting is part of healthy living._ However, if you have to adapt to the point of abandoning your core strengths to get the job done on a daily basis, you'll often find yourself in a stressful situation.

Turn to page 18 in your report. This section provides a comparison of your Core and Adapted Graphs. Again, your Core Style will not generally change significantly, but your adapted graph is a snapshot of how you are having to adapt to succeed, and it can change dramatically based on the signals sent by your environment. On pages 21–22 of your report, you will find an interpretation of the differences between your Core and Adapted Graph that can help you answer the questions below. In looking at your unique graphs, side by side, and the information on pages 21–22, answer the following questions and share what you've learned with those on your team.

---

1. Is there a significant difference in your Core Style Graph and your Adapted Style Graph? (Any plot points moving more than 30 percent up or down and/or crossing the Energy Line are significant.)

2. If so, in what areas do you have to adapt the most, and is the adaptation causing you anxiety or stress?

3. For those adaptations that are outside your control, to whom should you communicate this information?

All of us adapt to some degree, but some people feel that to succeed they need to adapt significantly from their natural God-given strengths. That can spell the difference between harmony or discord with yourself and others on your team.

SHARING YOUR GRAPHS WITH YOUR TEAM

The insights you have gained from this section—whether they're personal, spiritual, historical, or present-day reflections—can reveal the mask you are wearing and help you take it off, helping you to lead from your strengths. We strongly encourage you to humble yourself, open your heart and life to others on your team, and let them know the real you.

Chapter Eleven
Rolling on the River

IN THIS CHAPTER, we are going to walk you through what your Leading From Your Strengths® report says about how you communicate with others and how others should communicate with you. We will also deal with perceptions, how you see yourself and how others see you.

The truths you are about to learn affect all your relationships, not just those of your team. We need the ability to recognize the different strengths of each person on the team but also to understand each person's limitations and how to use our strengths to compensate for those limitations. All this becomes easier to see as we examine the

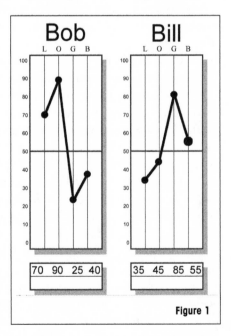

Figure 1

graphs of Bob and Bill, two elders from a church we worked with not long ago. First, let's look at their graphs and begin to discover who they are and how they will interact on their ministry team.

Bob's Core Style includes a high Otter, high Lion, low Golden Retriever, and low Beaver. Bill's Core Style includes a high Golden Retriever, high Beaver, low Otter, and low Lion. From what you have learned so far, you can see that they have different behavioral styles, and you can probably predict some of the conflict that is inevitable between the two. Inevitable, that is, unless they understand their different strengths and commit to a process of blending those strengths to make their relationship and their ministry team better.

Look at Bob's Core Style Graph first. Bob scored 70 percent on the Lion scale. If you look at the Lion descriptions on the far left column of the continuum (figure 2), and note which descriptors fall around that plot point (outlined with the circle on the column), you will see that his score would correlate with the following traits: Ambitious, Strong-Willed, Determined, and Competitive.

Now let's look at his ministry teammate, Bill's, score. Bill is beneath the Energy Line with a score of 35 percent on the Lion scale. This means that he would tend to exhibit the following behaviors (outlined with the square on the continuum): Cooperative, Low-Keyed, Understanding, and Cautious.

The results of Bob and Bill's assessments tell us that these two men would approach problems and challenges in an entirely different way. Though they both are committed to solving problems and meeting challenges, Bob and Bill have two different styles with corresponding strengths. On their ministry team these two styles have areas of predictable conflict. For example, Bob is aggressive, charging into the situation and taking on the problems and challenges boldly. Bill, on the other hand, will naturally take a step back, think about the problems and challenges, and even take time out to get more information before making a decision.

Moving to the next plot point on the Core Graph, the Otter scale, we see that Bob scores high at 90 percent. Looking at the descriptor column under Otter on the continuum, we see that the characteristics associated with this level on the graph (highlighted with the circle) are Inspiring, Enthusiastic, Demonstrative, and Persuasive. This contrasts again with Bill's score of 45 percent on the Otter scale. Adjectives that describe Bill (noted with the square) are Factual, Calculating, Skeptical, and Logical. This represents a wide difference in styles between Bob's and Bill's approaches to trusting people and information as well as how they attempt to influence others. For example, Bob will naturally trust someone asking for help, and Bill will be more skeptical. This could cause conflict between them on the elder board when making such decisions.

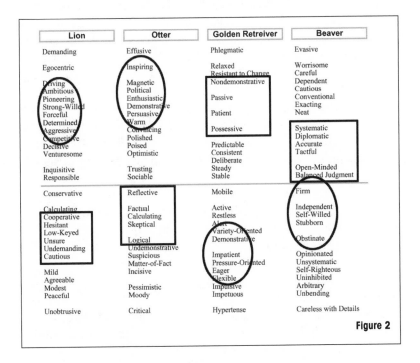

Lion	Otter	Golden Retreiver	Beaver
Demanding	Effusive	Phlegmatic	Evasive
Egocentric	Inspiring	Relaxed	Worrisome
		Resistant to Change	Careful
Driving	Magnetic	Nondemonstrative	Dependent
Ambitious	Political		Cautious
Pioneering	Enthusiastic	Passive	Conventional
Strong-Willed	Demonstrative		Exacting
Forceful	Persuasive	Patient	Neat
Determined	Warm		
Aggressive	Convincing	Possessive	Systematic
Competitive	Polished		Diplomatic
Decisive	Poised		Accurate
Venturesome	Optimistic	Predictable	Tactful
		Consistent	
		Deliberate	
Inquisitive	Trusting	Steady	Open-Minded
Responsible	Sociable	Stable	Balanced Judgment
Conservative	Reflective	Mobile	Firm
Calculating	Factual	Active	Independent
Cooperative	Calculating	Restless	Self-Willed
Hesitant	Skeptical	Alert	Stubborn
Low-Keyed		Variety-Oriented	
Unsure	Logical	Demonstrative	Obstinate
Undemanding	Undemonstrative		
Cautious	Suspicious	Impatient	Opinionated
	Matter-of-Fact	Pressure-Oriented	Unsystematic
Mild	Incisive	Eager	Self-Righteous
Agreeable		Flexible	Uninhibited
Modest	Pessimistic	Impulsive	Arbitrary
Peaceful	Moody	Impetuous	Unbending
Unobtrusive	Critical	Hypertense	Careless with Details

Figure 2

The next plot point on the Core Graph is the Golden Retriever. This characteristic deals primarily with how people deal with change and the pace of activity they prefer in their lives. Here Bob's score is 25 percent, while Bill's score is 85 percent. On the continuum under the Golden Retriever scale, Bob (the circle) is described as Demonstrative, Impatient, Eager, and Flexible. Bill (the square) would be seen as Nondemonstrative, Passive, Patient, and Possessive. Just reading the words that describe them reveals the great difference in their styles. Bob's natural tendency is to accept change quickly, always pushing the team to move forward. This almost certainly will conflict with Bill's steady, deliberate, cautious approach to change. When it comes to the pace of life and dealing with change, Bob is in the fast lane, and Bill has his foot on the brake.

Finally, the Beaver scale, the last plot point on the Core Graph, shows that Bob scores 40 percent, while Bill scores 55 percent. When it comes to following established rules and procedures and being good with details, Bob (the circle) is going to be Firm, Independent, Self-Willed, and Stubborn. Bill's characteristics (noted in the square) are Systematic, Diplomatic, Accurate, and Tactful. On this scale both men fall close together and close to the Energy Line. Reading their descriptors carefully shows the potential for conflict between them although it is not as great as with the other scales. Bob is more likely to ignore the established rules to achieve a goal. For Bob, the way it's always been done before is unimportant. Bill, however, wants to know all the relevant facts and will look to past precedent in making decisions now.

The divergence in their styles reveals many areas where these two men could experience interpersonal conflict on their ministry team. Here is a simple example to show how this style difference could cause conflict.

Suppose the worship leader of their church comes to the elder board and shares an exciting new idea he's to supercharge worship. He has taken some of the congregation's favorite old hymns, rewritten them, and set them to new music. He would like to begin having the congregation sing them in worship on Sunday. Bob is immediately impressed and thinks it is a great idea. He lets the others on the elder board know it by giving a long, loud, and emotional discourse on why this idea should be implemented to stimulate the congregation to new heights of worship. For Bob, next Sunday can't come soon enough.

Bill has other ideas. He wants to stop and consider the idea and its implications. He would like to hear some of the songs before they are sung in church. Bill thinks a change like this would be better made at the beginning of the next calendar year, six months away!

Instant conflict unless Bob and Bill understand and value each other's God-given strengths. Once they do, they can see each other in a different, more positive, light. Disagreement is no longer seen as personal but something that can make the elder board's decision-making better and the team more effective. In fact, it can help Bob and Bill's personal relationship just as much as their ministry team. This is the goal of the Leading From Your Strengths® process.

We have discovered three important elements to interpersonal interaction that need to be remembered for more effective communication. **The first is that information is the greatest modifier of behavior. The second is that the source of information must be trusted and reliable. Third, people rarely change the way they like to receive information.** Therefore, it is the responsibility of the sender to adapt their communication in order to send it the way the receiver wants it. This is a new way of thinking for many and one of the biggest barriers to overcome in making communication more effective. We have found that not understanding these principles is a significant factor in ministry teams where communication has broken down and individuals are not working close to their full potential.

If possible, we strongly encourage all of your ministry team members to take the assessment and for the team to review the communication section of everyone's reports. Everyone around you might well understand how to communicate with you, but it is equally important to know how to communicate with others to be an effective team member and to build effective ministry teams.

How Can We Help You

Chapters 9 and 10 were designed to bring out the personal elements in your Leading From Your Strengths® report. In the remainder of this chapter we will be focusing on the interpersonal elements of your report. In these sections we want to:

1. Help you better understand how others should or shouldn't be communicating with you.
2. Help you discover how others on your ministry team like to be communicated with, identify specific reasons you may have difficulty communicating with them, and assist you in developing effective strategies for better communication with them.

It is only when we understand our strengths and weaknesses and the strengths and limitations of others that we can effectively communicate. By unlocking the doors to understanding and using the keys of communication, you and your ministry team are freed to become effective communicators and achieve your ministry goals.

"CHECKLIST FOR COMMUTATING" SECTION
OF YOUR ONLINE REPORT

Remember the third element we discussed earlier: People rarely change the way they like to receive information. Therefore, it is important for others to know what will create barriers in communicating with you. The same is true as you communicate with others. Find out how they prefer to be communicated with and do it in that manner. For example, some people like direct communication, without much elaboration; someone else might like you to go into great detail; and yet others need you to make sure to ask about their family or feelings in the beginning of a conversation.

Turn to page 8 of your report. This section identifies specific ways in which you like to be communicated with. Identifying these keys to communication and sharing them with others on your team can spell the difference between good and great communication. Read the do's listed in this section and answer the following questions:

---

1. What are the four statements that best describe the way you like to be communicated with?

2. Now, reread the four statements above. What trends do you see in the statements you selected? If there is a trend, could this hold a key to the way you see trusted and reliable information?

3. What are the most important communication key(s) that others should keep in mind when communicating with you?

If you turn to page 9 of your report, you will see a list of the specific things people should *not* do when communicating with you. Read these statements carefully and answer the following questions.

---

1. What are the four statements that best describe the way you do not like to be communicated with?

2. What trend do you see in these statements?

3. What is the one thing that everyone communicating with you should know from the statements you selected?

4. Who are the people in your sphere of influence (members of your team, your family or friends) that you will share this information with to help them better understand how to communicate with you?

As you think about your responses to the questions above, could areas of miscommunication you experience now be traced back to how others communicate with you in ways that are unproductive or ineffectual for you? This is why it is critically important for us to sort through and understand how others should communicate with us so that we can convey this information to those we regularly deal with.

"COMMUNICATING WITH OTHERS" SECTION
OF YOUR ONLINE REPORT

You probably don't have difficulty communicating with all the people on your ministry team, but it can be the one or two that you do have trouble communicating with that can offset any benefit from effective communication with others.

The best-case scenario is if all the members of your team have completed the Leading From Your Strengths® assessment. This would allow you and your other team members to share specific dos and don'ts from this section.

If you are communicating with someone who has not completed the Leading From Your Strengths® assessment, the following exercise is designed to help you identify the predominate behavioral styles you have the most difficulty communicating with and some specific tips to help you communicate more effectively with them. These tips and questions are designed to open your eyes to the obstacles you encounter in your day-to-day

COMMUNICATION TIPS	
When communicating with a **Lion**, a person who is ambitious, forceful, decisive, strong willed, independent, and goal oriented: • Be clear, specific, brief, and to the point. • Stick to business. • Be prepared with support material in a well-organized package. Factors that will create tension or dissatisfaction: • Talking about things that are not relevant to the issue. • Leaving loopholes or cloudy issues. • Appearing disorganized.	When communicating with an **Otter**, a person who is magnetic, enthusiastic, friendly, demonstrative, and political: • Provide a warm and friendly environment. • Don't deal with a lot of details; put them in writing. • Ask "feeling" questions to draw out their opinions or comments. Factors that will create tension or dissatisfaction: • Being curt, cold, or tight-lipped. • Controlling the conversation. • Dwelling on facts and figures, alternatives, or abstractions.
When communicating with a **Golden Retriever**, a person who is patient, predictable, reliable, steady, relaxed, and modest: • Begin with a personal comment; break the ice. • Present your case softly, in a nonthreatening manner. • Ask "how" questions to draw out their opinions. Factors that will create tension or dissatisfaction: • Rushing headlong into business. • Being domineering or demanding. • Forcing them to respond quickly to your objectives.	When communicating with a **Beaver**, a person who is dependent, neat, conservative, perfectionist, careful, and compliant: • Prepare your case in advance. • Stick to business. • Be accurate and realistic. Factors that will create tension or dissatisfaction: • Being giddy, casual, informal, or loud. • Pushing too hard or being unrealistic with deadlines. • Being disorganized or messy.

interactions with the different behavioral styles. Some of these styles, especially when they are the opposite of your style, may cause you the greatest difficulty in effectively communicating.

What we have provided in the chart is a basic overview of communication tips for dealing with different behavioral styles. While reading the chart, think about the behavioral type you have the most difficult time communicating with.

Now that you have identified the most difficult style for you to communicate with, answer the following questions.

---

1. Which dominant personality style do you think you have the most trouble communicating with? What are the elements of that style that cause you the most frustration?

2. What are a few specific strategies from the tips listed for that style in the chart you can use to avoid tension and increase effective communication with them?

It is important that we take these strategies to heart whether it is with our ministry teams, our families, our friends, or the wide variety of people with whom we come into contact every day. We can use this information to communicate with those in our sphere of influence who have differing styles. By doing so, we can begin to break down the barriers of communication that limit the impact of our ministry.

"PERCEPTIONS" SECTION OF YOUR ONLINE REPORT

Based on our unique behavioral style, we are constantly sending all kinds of signals through the way we interact with other people. How we see ourselves can be different from someone observing and interacting with us who may have a different style. What we see as our greatest strength may be perceived by someone else to be a frustrating weakness. This can be accentuated when we are under pressure. We need to know how others see us in order to create a framework for effective communication.

Turn to page 16 in your report. This section identifies how you see yourself and how others might see you under moderate and extreme pressure. As you read and reflect on this information, think about how others could misunderstand your style and how this might inhibit your effectiveness on the team. With this in mind, answer the following questions:

---

1. What specific insights have you gained from these perceptions?

2. What can you do to take control when you find yourself under stress?

3. Are there any perceptions that you see as roadblocks to your being a productive team member?

4. If so, what steps can you take to remove the obstacles?

Perhaps the most important elements to this section of your report are the words that others may use to describe you when you are under moderate or extreme pressure. These are the signals you send to others that create barriers of communication, usually at the time you need to be communicating the most effectively. By understanding the miscommunication that can happen because of these perceptions, you can avoid the resulting conflict that can sap your energy and make it difficult to reach your ministry goals.

A CHALLENGE TO YOU

One of the keys to success for a ministry team is for its members to adapt their communication with others so it is effective and enables the team to reach its potential. This requires that we be *intentional* in our interactions with others. Communication is a two-way street. To build the environment of trust that our ministry teams need to do this, we must understand our own strengths and weaknesses, understand and value the strengths of our fellow team members, and be committed to blending the strengths and complementing the weaknesses. Only then will we be able to communicate effectively. Failure to do this inhibits our ability to communicate with those who need to hear it most—our teammates. The challenge to you is to consider what measures you need to take to express to those around you how you want to be communicated with. In turn, your responsibility is to find out how others prefer to be communicated with and then do it. If you do both of these things, you can expect your ministry team to prosper, at least in the development of the relationships on the team. Everyone on your ministry team wins, and God is honored.

Chapter Twelve

The Leading From Your Strengths® Wheel

PICTURE A BEAUTIFUL CONFERENCE ROOM with overstuffed executive chairs for everyone in the room. It was our privilege to conduct a staff training day for the key leadership team of a large church. Sitting down with teams is something we love to do as the teaching team for Leading From Your Strengths®, but that day there wasn't a great deal of love in the room. Friction, yes. Unresolved issues, absolutely. Yet a wise senior pastor had decided things wouldn't get better by just doing more of the same, which is a wise thing for any group to realize!

Before the training session, each person of staff had taken the Leading From Your Strengths® assessment, and we'd already spent most of the morning going through each person's report. Then came a dramatic moment in our time together, and it came when we looked at one of the most helpful sections of the Leading From Your Strengths® report. As we went through the Wheel at the end of the report, the Lord used this visual tool that morning to open eyes and hearts and even break down walls.

A FIRST LOOK AT YOUR STRENGTHS WHEEL

Before we look at what happened with this particular team, let's get a basic understanding of the Wheel at the end of your Leading From Your Strengths® report. This page takes the Core and Adapted Graphs and distills them into two plot points on the Wheel. The dot represents the Core Style, and the star represents the Adapted

Style. In this chapter we will help you understand the significance of these plot points, depending on where they plot on the Wheel. We will also cover how to use the Wheel page in a team-building session to gain an understanding of the team's natural and adapted tendencies of behavior.

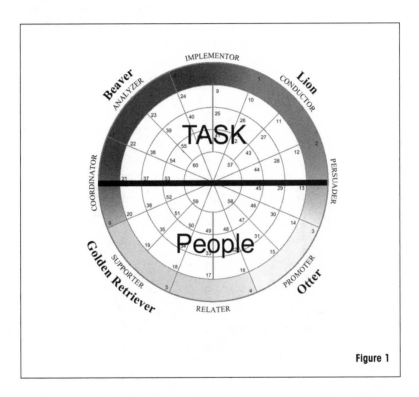

Figure 1

Take a look at the blank Wheel without someone's individual scores inserted (see figure 1). You'll notice the four animals around the outside of the circle that represent the four key behavioral styles we've covered in this book. In figure 1 you will see a bold line running through the center of the Wheel from left to right. We have inserted this line in figure 1 to help you see how to interpret the points on the Wheel. You'll also notice we have inserted a word in bold at the top and bottom of the Wheel. At the top of the Wheel is the word *task* and at the bottom, *people*. When a point is above this line, it indicates that the person will be more task oriented than people oriented. If the plot were on the bottom side of the Wheel, the person would be more people oriented as opposed to task oriented.

Now look at figure 2 and you'll also notice another bold line running from the top to the bottom of the Wheel. The word *slower* has been added to the left edge of the Wheel, and *faster* to the right side of the Wheel. This denotes those who like to move at a faster pace being plotted to the right of the line, and those who would naturally want to move slower plotted to the left of the line.

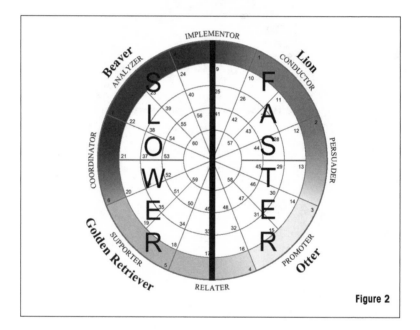

Figure 2

In figure 3 you'll notice that there are a series of rings starting at the inner circle and growing as they move toward the outside band of the Wheel. As you look at your core dot and your adapted star, the more they move toward the middle of the Wheel—toward that inner circle—the more plot points you have above the Energy Line. Blending more of the four behavioral tendencies together indicates that you're more flexible than your behavior is. The further you move toward the outside of the Wheel, the fewer plot points you have above the Energy Line and the more rigid you will see that behavior.

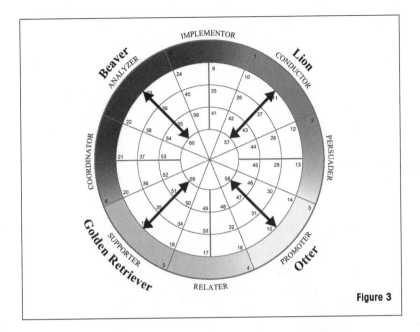

Figure 3

NEXT STEPS IN UNDERSTANDING YOUR WHEEL

To explain this further, let's look at a sample report from one of the twelve people in the room that morning in the large church conference room.

In figure 4 you'll see Pastor Alan's Wheel. At a glance, you get the picture that Alan is definitely people oriented! In fact, if he scored any higher on the Golden Retriever, he'd be outside the circle! Both his dot (representing his core strengths and style) and his star (representing his adapted strengths and style) are close together; basically he keeps people in mind and tends to be slower paced. In everyday ministry, these Golden Retriever traits are a great help to Alan, who is the pastor overseeing hospital visitation and assimilating new members.

In Alan's case, there is little differentiation or distance between his dot (Core Style) and star (Adapted Style). With many other people you will see a marked difference in where the dot and star fall on the Wheel. Just as in our discussion of Core and Adapted Graphs, looking at the direction the star is moving from the dot can indicate how you're adapting and to what degree your Core Style differs from your adapted. Alan certainly projects a great deal of warmth and concern for others, both core and adapted, which shows up on his Wheel. But you notice he feels that he needs to speed up a little, and that is what is pushing his adapted star toward the right side of the Wheel.

Alan now knows why he feels that things are going a little too fast at times. And while gaining this additional picture of Alan's core and adapted strengths was helpful to him personally, it's how this Wheel leads to a breakthrough as a team that proved life-changing that morning.

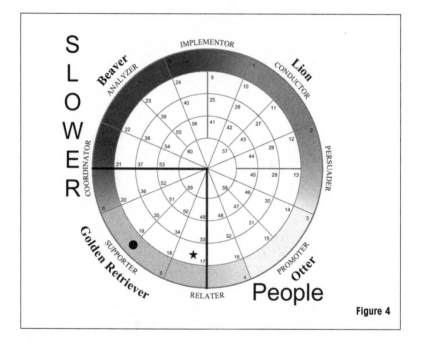

Figure 4

PLOTTING YOUR ENTIRE TEAM USING
YOUR STRENGTHS WHEEL

Ask any counselor and he'll tell you that it's much more powerful when the counselee in the room sees something significant for himself or herself, rather than having it pointed out to them. Almost without exception, when we work with teams, it's when we get to the Strengths Wheel that lights, whistles, and bells go off for the team as they get the picture of who's in their raft.

Typically in team training we'll have each person on the team come up to a whiteboard or flip chart at the front of the room and use a marker to draw a dot (or Core Style score) on a large, blank Wheel. As an example of what it looks like when an entire ministry team places their core strengths dots on a team Wheel, figure 5 shows eleven out of the twelve pastor's dots from Alan's teammembers' individual Wheels.

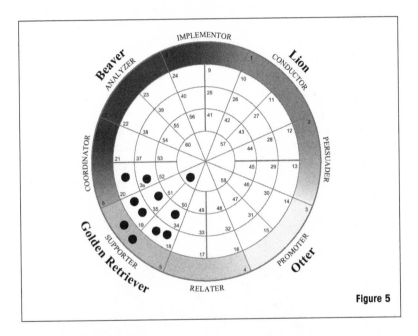

Figure 5

From looking at all the dots that represent this ministry team, take a guess what kind of church visitors discover when they walk in the door of this church. With nearly every staff person high on the Golden Retriever/Beaver scale and all clustered in the people/slower area of the Wheel, if you guessed "This is a warm, sincere, people-oriented church," you'd be right! As a staff of Golden Retrievers, no one had been at the church less than six years (and some as long as eighteen years). They had greeters and welcome classes, encouragement cards in each pew, world-class socials on Wednesday night, and Sunday night suppers each week! But you'll notice, I said nearly every staff member's circle fell in the same area.

There was one dramatic exception to the "we only speak Golden Retriever here" staff. His name was Mark, and he was the senior pastor who had set up our meeting.

Let's take a look at this ministry team's Wheel with the twelfth staff person's score plotted on the Wheel (figure 6) and add in the fact that this final dot represents a senior pastor who had been at the church less than two years.

For those reading this book who have worked with groups, the potential for misunderstanding and hurt feelings that instantly comes to mind when you've got a huddle of Golden Retrievers and a leader who's an off-the-chart Lion-Otter is tremendous. It wasn't just potential problems this team faced. Pick almost any area—from staff reviews, to sermon series, to the way outreach was done, to the way the kitchen should run at potlucks—and you had someone who liked to move fast, make changes, and take charge, leading a herd of people worried about how those changes would affect themselves and the congregation and who liked the status quo! (That's why the average person had been there almost a decade!)

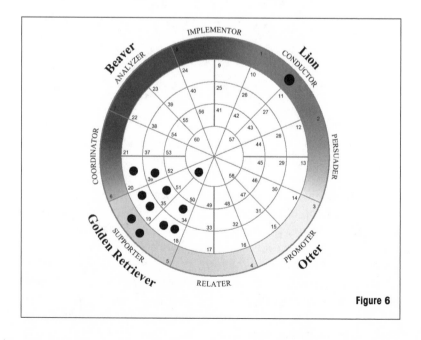

Figure 6

Hiring Mark to come in and initiate changes was something the leaders of the church did purposefully. They'd had a senior pastor for years who fit with the staff, and they were looking for someone with more drive, more energy, more new ideas. However, only problems were resulting, not progress. But things were about to change.

I've mentioned several times that a paradigm shift took place that morning. Actually, it was more like geologic plates under the earth shifting. For almost two years this group of Golden Retrievers had suffered in loyal silence but had screamed out their frustration at the new Lion senior pastor in nonverbal ways. Not only that, but passive-aggressive responses to all his changes were the norm, not the exception. (Meaning, the more the Lion roared to speed up changes, the slower and more cautious the Retriever/Beaver implemented his orders!) It is important to understand that they were not being obstinate, but they were afraid to miss the expectations of the Lion and suffer the consequences.

Unfortunately, the senior pastor had been so intent on initiating change, he hadn't invested the time needed to build the kind of emotional equity with his staff that would help them accept and implement change. Meeting with us was the first thing they'd done as a staff to build a closer team, and two years of frustration came to a head after the senior pastor went to the board and put his dot on the team's Wheel. After he sat down, there was almost dead silence in the room. Without saying a word, as each person looked at their team's Wheel, it was like the elephant in the room was suddenly visible. After a long time of silence (hard to do when there is tension in the room, but a good team-building skill to learn), we asked a single question.

Addressing the question to Mark, the senior pastor, we asked, "Mark, do you ever feel lonely out there?" The senior pastor didn't answer. After two years of feeling like he was in ministry alone, his head just dropped, and he let out an involuntary, audible sigh. As you might imagine, with a room full of Golden Retrievers, seeing the vulnerability and hurt on their senior pastor's face was all it took for the entire room to instantly rally around Mark! Forget what we had planned for the rest of our time together. What took place when that team saw themselves on that Wheel opened up a discussion that turned into a time of honest sharing. That time of sharing turned into a time of asking forgiveness. And that tearful time of forgiveness turned into a time of prayer and planning that resulted in those people leaving the room feeling connected like a team as never before.

We're not saying that every team will experience as dramatic a shift as this when they plot out each person's scores. However, it is often eye-opening at least, and life changing at best, when people really see the team God has assembled.

You can download the Strengths Wheel Guide which details the process of working a team through the Strengths Wheel exercise that we used with Mark's church. Do this by going to www.leadingfromyourstrengths.com and clicking on Free Downloads.

Remember how we began this book, referring to 1 Corinthians 12, and noting how "God has placed the parts, each one of them, in the body just as He wanted" (v. 18). While it's certainly not the only way, the Strengths Wheel is a powerful way from a God-given strengths perspective to see those God has placed in your raft. In light of that, here are five questions to ask yourself and your team when you place yourselves on a Strengths Wheel.

FIVE QUESTIONS TO ASK YOURSELF AND YOUR TEAM

1. What areas of overlap do we have in our team? (Are most of you on the fast side of the Wheel, or clustered near the center of the Wheel, or all at the far edges?)
2. What are the open areas on our team? (Is there an absence of Otters? No one sharing Beaver or Lion traits? No one on the fast side of the Wheel?)
3. What does this Wheel show us as a team that we can celebrate and thank the Lord for?
4. What does this Wheel show us that we can work on to be more balanced or united as a team?
5. If we added in everyone's adapted scores (the stars on your Leading From Your Strengths® Wheel), what tendencies or insights can we gain as well?

Using Your Strengths Wheel as a Key
to Future Staffing Needs

Many of you may have already jumped ahead to other ways to use your Strengths Wheel as a team. For example, this is a wonderful tool for seeing where people's core and adapted strengths are and then positioning people with tasks that fit their core gifts and abilities the best. For example, are there members of your team who are having to make major adaptations (their dots and stars are far apart on their Wheel) and they could be given tasks that fit their core strengths more closely?

Another team-building benefit of using your Strengths Wheel can be illustrated in one of the downstream discussions we had with the ministry team from the large church. Once they had gotten a picture of just who was in their raft, they had a tremendous discussion about what strengths the next staff person they brought on should have.

For example, as good as this church with a room full of Retrievers was at making people feel welcome, they knew from experience that there was a huge gap in follow-through with projects (meaning all the Golden Retrievers had a hard time saying no and often overpromised things and struggled with prioritizing). Perhaps they needed someone on board with more Beaver follow-through skills who could give them Beaver lessons! Also, because of what they learned about themselves, suddenly the Otter types they had interviewed and passed over in the past suddenly were seen in a different light. With so many on staff so serious and slow to change, they realized that perhaps a children's education director with an Otter's energy and new ideas for recruitment might not be such a bad thing after all.

While we could write an entire book on selecting new staff members (and we will one day soon!), the insights gained through your Strengths Wheel is a wonderful way to see the strengths of others in a new light and to shed light on holes or areas of strength you don't have on your existing team. If you are a leader who is responsible for selecting and placing new staff, you will find a step-by-step guide to using the Leading From Your Strengths® assessment in selecting additional staff on our Web site, www.leadingfromyourstrengths.com under Free Downloads.

Finally, not only resolving conflict and hiring can be aided by a look at this Wheel, but the Wheel is such a natural platform for raising and talking through current issues and problems, it's a great staff retention tool! It's one thing to find great people to minister with; it's another thing to keep them together. While no one wanted to mention it, in the frank discussion this ministry team had, several of the Golden Retrievers had lost hope that things would ever change and were actually thinking of leaving the church. That's after years together! By getting on the same page, they were able not only to fill open spots with needed strengths, but they also could see value in working through issues with existing staff.

ONE FINAL THOUGHT FROM A SPIRITUAL PERSPECTIVE

When you think about our Lord, did he have any Lion characteristics? (He was called the "Lion of Judah.") Did he have any Otter traits? (He was comfortable around groups, full of life and energy and expressive words.) Did Jesus demonstrate any Golden Retriever traits? (He grieved over the death of a friend, built a close-knit team, and was full of compassion.) And did he live out any Beaver traits? (He followed the standards established by God, finished what he started, and spoke words that were accurate and full of truth.)

The Lord could do the most loving thing when someone most needed it. What's more, when we see how people fall on this Wheel, it again takes us back to that 1 Corinthians 12 picture of a whole body. If you'll remember, when it came to spiritual gifts, like a human body with many parts, all are important, and all have been placed in the body of Christ by divine design.

By application, we are not all Lions, but we need their Christlike strength of character and willingness to tackle tough issues. We're not all Otters, but being full of joy and life and relationship skills reflects his love for others. We're not all Golden Retrievers, but having people on our ministry teams who are caring and compassionate, good listeners and healers helps reflect the Savior's heart. And thank the Lord for the Beaver types, who also reflect our Lord's perseverance and patience, and his willingness to dot i's and cross t's (biblically, "jots and tittles") and complete his work with an "It is finished."

Chapter Thirteen
Putting All You've Learned into Practice

★

IT'S BEEN OUR PRIVILEGE to be your guides in this Leading From Your Strengths® process for building close-knit ministry teams. As we conclude this book, we'd like to do several things. First, we'll take one last summary look at several of the key points found in this book. Then we'll ask you to act on some of what you've learned by scheduling time with your ministry team— sometime during the next five business days—to sit down and talk through the ideas and insights you've gained in this book. We'll then make some closing recommendations for further study and reflection, answer some of the most often asked follow-up questions we field at live training events.

ONE LAST FLYOVER TO HIGHLIGHT
KEY POINTS FROM THIS BOOK

We know that reading a book is and should be a personal experience. As such, we hope you already have your own "highlight film" of key statements or insights from your online report and various chapters—items that have particularly hit home with you in relation to your ministry team. But by way of summary and reminder, let's do one last "flyover" of some of the core teaching points that make up the Leading From Your Strengths® process.

First, we began with a hopeful look at three lives and three ministry outcomes that were decidedly, positively different because of working through the material you've now learned from this book. That's the first thing we pray you've picked up in every chapter of the book. Namely, *we genuinely believe your team can grow closer and accomplish more than ever before.*

We then looked at how by divine design, Almighty God himself is the One who places the members of his body "just the way he desires" (1 Corinthians 12). That includes placing us with people who are different from us in their approach to life and ministry. (We're not all eyes or ears in the body of Christ.) Differences then are part of what can make a ministry team most effective in building up the body and reaching out to others. But that doesn't mean that blending differences happens automatically or without effort.

In chapters 4–8, we shared *four predictable problems, four inevitable transition points,* that every ministry team will face. These four transition points can either become trials that lead a team onto the rocks or experiences that mold you into a close-knit team and propel you forward. These four challenges involve the way people approach problems either aggressively or passively; whether they look at information in a trusting way or are more naturally careful and skeptical when dealing with people and facts; how people react to change and the pace of activity in their lives and whether they are fast paced or slow paced; and finally, whether tasks and standard procedures take precedence over spontaneity, creativity, and thinking outside the box.

After looking at these predictable areas of group conflict, we then had you focus on your own God-given strengths by working through your Leading From Your Strengths® report. We had you look and reflect on several of the major sections of your report, such as your General Characteristics, Value to the Team, Communication Style, and Ideal Environment. We then shared the important insights captured in the Core and Adapted Graphs in your report and ended with a look at the Leading From Your Strengths® Wheel and how you can get a picture of your entire team by using this tool.

Armed with all that information, it's time to move from theory to practice and from information to application. In short, it's time for you to take the insights and learning you've gained from this book and your report and share them with your ministry team.

It's Time for Your Ministry Team to Meet

In our work with teams over the years, we've seen a consistent outcome. Those people who share what they've learned in reading this material or attending a seminar with others, particularly within a short time after learning these principles, see more short- and long-term change in their ministries. Our goal at seminars is to challenge people to pick a day, within five business days of going through the seminar (or putting down this book), to meet with your ministry team. Ideally, each member of your team has read this book, taken their online report, and completed the Leading From Your Strengths® process.

Draw up your own action plan for talking through the four transition points and how they apply to you, sharing key ideas and insights from each person's report, the Core and Adapted Graphs, and Strengths Wheel. In many cases you'll learn more about those you minister with in that first meeting than you may have in months or even years of working side by side! You'll see their heart and gifts in a clearer way, as well as understand their ideal environment and what motivates them more personally.

Before you have your meeting, please e-mail us, and our team will indeed pray for you that your meeting time will become a life-changing event for everyone on your team. Then let us know how your meeting went. E-mail us at feedback@leadingfromyour strengths.com. Please let us know in your e-mail if we can share your team story—the successes or challenges you've faced together—with others. Whether it's from our Web site or in a training session with others, your story could help another team succeed at connecting, relating, and heading off issues.

Questions We're Often Asked

At live training events, two questions are asked again and again. The first is, "How do I get additional Leading From Your Strengths® assessments for family members or friends?" You can order individual online assessments for friends, family, or others you minister with (support staff, elders or deacons, etc.) at our Web site, www.leadingfromyourstrengths.com. By visiting our site, you'll be able to order additional reports like the one you took, or a marriage or family version of the online report as well.

If you do consulting or corporate chaplain work in secular businesses, you'll find a workplace version of our online report for corporate settings. For those of you who do counseling or consulting, being able to have your clients or entire teams take the Leading From Your Strengths® online assessment can be a tremendous benefit for them and a help to you.

Finally, if you're serious about hiring or adding the right person for your ministry team, be sure to look on our Web site at Position Insights. This online, interactive tool is specifically designed for groups (like search committees or boards) or individuals to come up with the core strengths and style needed to fill a particular position on a team.

A CLOSING CHALLENGE TO GO DEEPER BY WORKING THROUGH A NATIONAL CERTIFICATION PROGRAM

We can't encourage you enough to take your report, your book, and the insights you've learned from both, and share that with important people on your team and in your life. For some, perhaps you're already convinced that the Leading From Your Strengths® process is something you'd like to champion in your church, workplace, or community.

If you'd like to go much deeper in understanding how the report was constructed, being able to read the graphs and Wheel more accurately, and become equipped to facilitate a live team-building session for your ministry team or others, we encourage you to visit our Web site to learn about becoming a certified Leading From Your Strengths® trainer. We are developing a program to train everyone on your ministry team or selected individuals from your staff. By visiting our Web site and clicking on "Becoming a Certified Trainer," you will get an update on when the certification program will begin.

For each of us reading this book, it's crucial to remind ourselves to number our days and make the most of each hour. It may seem that our time of service on our ministry team will last forever, but just ask someone who's recently retired how quickly the years went. Just like watching our kids grow so quickly, we need to invest time and energy into making our time of ministry here on earth as positive and effective for Christ as it can possibly be.

It's our prayer that your ministry team will be stronger and more effective than before because you took your assessment and worked through this book. May the Lord bless, keep, and guide you each day until the great day of His coming, and may you always lead from your strengths in serving the King of all kings.

John Trent, Ph.D.   Rodney Cox
The Leading From Your Strengths® Teaching Team